Our Journey is not an Accident, would not have been a possibility without my Lord and Savior. Who made pathways where relationships could dawn and lessons would be learned.

Thank you,
Peach, Batch, Luke, Adam, Matt Murda, Matthew Prescott, Dan & Dave(IN2Action), D. Arinder, and Grace for the insight and support throughout the process. Lastly, my Westbow team: Hanna, Brady, Rebecca, Bob, & Heather S. for the spark.

Sincerely appreciative,
D. R.

OUR JOURNEY IS NOT AN ACCIDENT

FAILURES DON'T DEFINE US. THEY REFINE US!

D.R. BIRCH

WESTBOW
PRESS®

A DIVISION OF THOMAS NELSON
& ZONDERVAN

WestBow Press books may be ordered through booksellers or by contacting:

WestBow Press
A Division of Thomas Nelson & Zondervan
1663 Liberty Drive
Bloomington, IN 47403
www.westbowpress.com
1 (866) 928-1240

Because of the dynamic nature of the Internet, any web addresses or links contained in this book may have changed since publication and may no longer be valid. The views expressed in this work are solely those of the author and do not necessarily reflect the views of the publisher, and the publisher hereby disclaims any responsibility for them.

Any people depicted in stock imagery provided by Getty Images are models, and such images are being used for illustrative purposes only. Certain stock imagery © Getty Images.

Anchor photo courtesy of David Batchler

Scripture quotations taken from The Holy Bible, New International Version® NIV® Copyright © 1973 1978 1984 2011 by Biblica, Inc. TM. Used by permission. All rights reserved worldwide.

ISBN: 978-1-9736-9293-5 (sc)
ISBN: 978-1-9736-9292-8 (e)

Print information available on the last page.

WestBow Press rev. date: 08/31/2020

SCRIPTURES REFERENCED

CHRISTIAN GUIDE
PROVERBS 3:5-6, 6:2-3, 16:9, 18:21, 23: 3-4
JAMES 1:2, 1:19
1ST PETER 5:7
2ND PETER 3:9
JOHN 14:27
ISAIAH 61:7
1ST CORINTHIANS 13:7
ROMANS 3:23, 8:28

SKEPTIC INDEX
2ND CORINTHIANS 7:10, 9:8
COLLOSIANS 1:17, 3:23
PHILLIPIANS 4:13
1ST THESSALONIANS 5:17
GENESIS 2:18
2ND TIMOTHY 2:23
PROVERBS 16:25
GALATIANS 5:19-20
EPHESIANS 5:31
1ST SAMUEL 16:7
HEBREWS 12:27
1ST JOHN 3:6, 4:16

NAVIGATION FOR THE JOURNEY
INDEX GUIDE & CONTENT ITINERARY

Our Journey has used a passive voice, as well as, a soft academic tone. Ensuing to create a personal conversation with each reader. In addition, to respect the privacy of those related to situations.

INDEX GUIDE & CONTENT ITINERARY

NOTE: Anyone reading this book without an understanding of who Christ is and assurance of salvation, please begin with skeptic perspective and continue to the moments with the Highly Exalted. Then the Christian perspective if this stirs something inside you. I hope it does just that. Read from the last page of the book forward.

CHRISTIAN PROLOGUE

The impact I'm hoping this book achieves is an acceptance of your purpose and your full self; Thus, releasing you from captivity. This will take a steadfastness as you enter trivial destinations of reflection in your mind about past and present. Rest assured, there is comfort with God's promise. After reading *Our Journey is not an Accident,* my hope is everyone will have a true revelation of just how much God loves all of us. A love only possible by what His son did for us on the cross. I also hope readers receive a calming confirmation that we are more than ok, despite trials and difficult situations encountered consistently. Even your grandpa Ed can find comfort and peace, if he chooses to gracefully exchange hunting for a pardon, granted to the neighbor's cat and ceases smoking.

God put on my heart some time ago, how much of an issue a large majority of the Christian population is facing in today's world. Cognitively, we seem to be lacking an awareness that people cannot obtain a life of perfection in a finite vessel. Only one conquered death, and we are trapped in a shell that's ridden with sin. I encourage you to refrain from lofty expectations to be like Christ and accept being Christ like. Sin affects everyone and will continue executing carnage upon humanity until the Lord returns. Until then lighten up, take a breath, and stop fretting about the call you didn't make to Karen, when she received the news of a health concern. Trust, Karen isn't pondering, why you didn't call her either. Resist terrorizing yourselves, due to the less than kind gestures you gave freely to the trash collectors when the act of tossing your trash containers, recklessly, caused a tumbling of tin containers and residual trash that finished in the yard, three houses down your street. When God accepted us into His family, we received a wonderful promise. 2000 years ago, an exemption from sin came to be through, Jesus. Shedding his blood and sacrificing His life abolished any other sacrifices deemed required to cleanse us of sin. Although, this doesn't mean sin is excused just paid for by our friend, Jesus. It still hurts, no doubt, even stings a bit more. Due to the conviction of the Holy Spirit living in us. It's a good pain to endure, because, grieving the Holy Spirit is awful and the absence of pain delivered from conviction when commencing to sin is a heavier burden to bear.

Our Journey is not an Accident takes the reader on a tour, reminding Christians of a promise, written millenniums ago. A promise of comfort through all of our trials and failures along the journey. Moreover, enhancing our maturity and keeps us from becoming lost. Through relatable affirmations, trials of overcoming obstacles, and circumstances involving emotional overflow in building faith and suffering grief. Reminding believers, of God's agape love that's unwavering towards Christians through the sacrifice and resurrection. Jesus, said pick up your cross and follow Him. I know it wasn't pick up your cross and hang on it. Jesus, declared, it's finished with His dying breath. The weight of our problems can be heavy when choosing to act with motives driven by the flesh, as I will attest. Disobeying what God declares right for us will result in disciplinary action but what we also forget is the domino effect of sin. Sin is contagious and can vicariously bring consequential measures upon others not even related to the deed in question, whatsoever. Proof of the ongoing trickle-down affect is available from the beginning, Adam & Eve.

I hope this book awards readers insight into relationships that hold true to God and His purpose for you. Creating a steadfast nature strong in the midst of learning curves. Inducing, a consciousness of God, confidence in Christ, and the comfort of the Holy One.

My prayer for anyone out there not able to recognize each new person that enters their path or impacts their life as a special creation made by God, is to receive a vision of innocence. We all should allow a person admission past the first impression and noticeable flaws according to worldly standards. Further, Lord I pray for a washing away of painful memories lingering, a knowledge of sin and it does not define us but allows you to refine us. Further lord, that sin is the root of all conflict, pain, and judgment holding them in bondage. Father blanket their souls with the calming assurance of your sovereignty in all things, Amen.

Christian Section 1

REFLECTIONS OF THE PROMISE

Testimonies

A FATHER'S PROMISE

A FATHER'S PROMISE

Testimonies

Trust! Trusting the person God made you to be. Belief, the gifts and tools you are equipped with can work towards success in your journey and assist others too. Understanding, might not be a strong characteristic for some, still trust in Him as your creator and father in heaven. Why is this so important? Faith produces power to endure and overcome. A trust should manifest about God's love that leaves you with little or no doubt your caretaking on life's journey. We who are called are blessed through discipline. We do the same for our children. So how much more so with your sovereign father in heaven is this done for you? It can be frustrating, how everything happens according to His will and the right time. However, the more we witness this occurrence, the security the promise produces decreases anxiety. I encourage conversing often with your father in heaven, claim His goodness, give Him glory, and keep your spiritual eyes and ears open. Listen to your father as He speaks to you through prayer, nature, and others. One of His many great names Immanuel, means He is with us. Also, since we know His way is true and just, shouldn't we just let go, and let God lead? How many situations of adversity must we overcome before we recognize His agape love for us?

Remember, God sees His son, Jesus when He sees us. The path to righteousness will have struggles and strife, inevitably. Therefore, focus on the price of the promise and the mercy bestowed upon us. Let go of the doubt and guilt and start giving thanks showing gratitude.

THE CALLING

I had the privilege of meeting a couple that had been members of their church for years. The lady, currently a teacher, for years at the church, educating Sunday school children happen to be responsible for at least half of the family income. As happy as this lady seemed with her calling at her church and life in the town where she resided with her husband and children; She still felt something inside her, a calling from a still small voice whispering she needed to move on.

Eventually, that urge convinced her of heeding the call elsewhere. She knew further growth in her spirituality was only going to come from making a change. Acceptance now becoming real inside her being. She sat down with her husband to have the difficult and scary conversation of jumping into the unknown journey; Conveying to her husband the plan to start a missionary type ministry. This would include an immense amount of travel hard on the family but would fulfill Gods calling as well.

This adventure would bless her with the ability to sing and play music for the Lord, something she loved dearly and felt closest, to the Lord, when doing so. She had always been drawn to the closeness she felt when writing songs of praise (I relate, wholeheartedly).

Her talents playing keyboard and recording tunes of worship also were ignited by the spirit enough to set fire alarms sounding off. Even with this strong love and passion for music of praise, anxiety manifested in the knowledge of just how much courage she needed. Which she felt a lacking, not only, in courage but a measure of faith. Honestly, her faith felt much smaller than even a mustard seed at times. Swaying the fruition of the move, came in problems uprooting the children and relocating to different schools, financial woes from travel and lacking income, and constricting pressure on all of the relationships that would need patience to resist conflict.

Much to her surprise, the choice to embrace the challenge and allow God solely to direct their paths would persevere. Leading her family upon a journey for God's purpose in her life despite the fears. Her husband, where men's first thoughts consist of protection and provision to characterize a husband or father. Succeeded fighting insecurity with the lords might. Achieving a new found faith and identity all his own, while keeping an unwavering commitment to support his wife.

Currently, this magnificent duo are worship leaders of the gospel and deliver music to multitudes of men through prison ministry. This family remains blessed to travel to a multitude of states, in this great country, sharing the word, and changing lives by introducing our savior Jesus Christ to many deprived of His love prior to their mission. Needless to say, God provided sufficiently for this couple and their children. Their faith and unwavering trust in the Lord rewarded blessings abundantly, all the while, supplying what was needed along the way.

Here is an example of a married couple battling fear and doubt in decisiveness to accept the blessing of entering their calling to fulfill God's purpose. In contrast to Jonah's story faltering to obey the Father wasn't an option. So many times God attempts to bless our steps of faithful service with a request to respond to God. However, many good christians miss these opportunities because of fear or complacency in their church and fellowship areas of life. Don't be fooled into that safety net of a going through the motions with little accountability or calls to action church.The safety your mistaken by might just be stalling out your calling down a better road. Lean on prayer and discernment of the circumstances and the motives of people involved. The promise has layers in it like deliverance, saving, blessing, and a purposeful intent to bring the goodness through everything.

STAYCATION

This is something we all can relate to because all of us, I presume, have experienced situations out of our control, believers and skeptics alike. For example, my family sets aside time for our annual vacation in May. Like usual saving was a must from January onward to reach our financial goal. We stood firm, through disciplines, such as not taking any personal days off from work to maximize monetary gain and increasing our savings. Some of you relate, to this type of regime, surely. Just to reach a point two weeks prior to departing for the Mexico vacation with a horrible and unforeseen tragic incident. Our beloved family pet of 5 years, a beautiful chocolate miniature pinscher, had an accident that broke his hip during a fall off the front porch that approximately lifted about 6 feet off the ground. This brought a hard decision to be made and one which created division within the family. I envisioned the enemy rejoicing for the opportunity for disruption. Faced with the options of surgery and a long recovery or euthanizing our dog from the veterinarian. After much deliberation, my wife convinced me to go along with surgery. Despite any notion of confidence, the outcome would produce results, of quality life, according to dog standards for Dew. However, we would inherit medical costs topping over $2000 that had us waving Good-bye to vacation and saying hello STAYCATION.

This undoubtedly brought about frustration and disappointment for all of us. Nevertheless, the decision was final but what we didn't realize at the time, this choice would eventually put us deep into a financial hole. Due to more costs forthcoming from additional visits for medications. Sour moods infested the family. The kids mad at us, my wife mad at me for lack of preparation for such events, and I held a nasty scowl permanently, as I thought quietly," why, God why?" The cold shoulders and bickering seemed endless until the air twisted with uplift, a variable, God only could have conjured amidst this awful and frustrating situation.

As it happened, we bumped into a dear friend we hadn't seen in many years. "Where and how does this pertain to the story," you ask? This occurred at the veterinarian hospital where the surgery for our canine pal, had been scheduled. Our friend, in lowly spirits and obviously needing to talk, she shared that her life had been a steady flow of speed bumps lately. She went through a breakup, among some other surprises of the unfriendly version which enhanced the stress and didn't seem to be a resolution, anytime soon. In reflection, the promise of God had us appear at the right time for our ole` friend, not for us, perhaps. We were still blessed to do God's work for a friend that was down and out. The blessing was birthed in our discouragement and her low point which magnified the beauty of Gods promise and declared the sovereignty of the lord, simultaneously. God used all of us, not in a ideal situation to bring forth encouragement for our friend and help change all mindsets involved. Our suffering in a selfish nature turned to outward compassion with the fruits of the spirit. At this juncture of my life, the Lord's promise came into focus.

God works like this all the time but in our consuming nature about what we need, we miss the chance to give God glory in these moments. The Lord even works for us when we make mistakes or fixate on our wish list because of His promise to His children. There is such peace you'll receive in realizing that everything has a purpose or reason that exists but only in God's sovereignty, truly understood. All we need to do is remember this and have faith. Sure, we might not like it but that wasn't the promise, anyway. The promise is that it will work for the greater good somehow, someday. We can kick our feet like we did, pondering a decision on our pet. We can even refuse like Jonah, to do what the Lord asks of us and head in the opposite direction ending up in a whale. Free will is ours in the course we take, but God is sovereign overall, nonetheless. Acceptance, of this fact, is a good thing for believers, because obedient demeanor despite the dilemma's complexities will bring peace. Just like our family decision to save our pet's life. If we would have chosen the vacation over the pet there would have been grief over the loss of our dog and a dark cloud looming above vacation resort. Instead, we listened to our hearts, with Spiritual discernment, and chose the harder path.

God loves us and wants to bless us along the better road. This will happen when consulting the Spirit and not the flesh. So, If we fall in line with His will, He will give you your heart's desires. Just know the promise remains unchanged by choices, right or wrong, or the level of intensity, His character is the reason. Moses was in the wilderness for forty-two years and Jonah in the belly of a whale just three days, nevertheless, God's will was served by both and it will be by you too.

PATIENCE FOR THE PUFFER

> ### 2ND PETER 3:9
>
> THE LORD IS NOT SLOW IN KEEPING HIS PROMISE, AS SOME UNDERSTAND SLOWNESS. HE IS PATIENT WITH YOU, NOT WANTING ANYONE TO PERISH, BUT EVERYONE TO COME TO REPENTANCE.

This scripture should be comforting and received by multitudes. First, the obvious is that God's time is not our time. The Lord lives outside of time giving us the chances allotted to receive our salvation. Do not be fooled that this is an open-ended invitation. One will never know how much time we are allotted, please, do not gamble. There is not any amount of sin that feeds the flesh worth your eternity in heaven.

Going deeper into the layers of the living word here reminds me of a friend who had turned his life around and began walking with the Lord. However, as time went by, he continued to struggle with smoking cigarettes. This lingered for months with much praying and effort in self-control. success in quitting this nasty habit still eluded my pal, the puffer. Mr. Music began to feel he had failed God and guilt started overtaking his heart because of not receiving a deliverance. I happened to be attending church when the spirit spoke to me. I was being urged to speak using this scripture in front of many brothers in Christ. I asked him to meditate on this verse and hopefully he would realize that God has knowledge of his trial and the Holy Spirit is working on him, in him and through him. He was maturing in many ways and that comfort should be found there. I also reminded him about his Father's patience concerning our salvation. Emphasizing, to not let the enemy add the weight of guilt or confusion when deciphering thoughts on our Father's love or what His main concerns consist of. We all battle with certain sins more than others. Stay faithful and keep the fight. In God's time not ours we all can find deliverance from our crutches and weaknesses of the flesh. Remember, if God's word declares patience when dealing with repentance, then how much more likely, is He to be patient with your battles to eliminate those sins that fall far beneath the importance of the soul.

FALLING IS NOT FAILING

ROMANS 3:23

WE ALL FALL SHORT OF THE GLORY OF GOD.

Christians are called to be Christ like, and Christ was and is perfect. Let us focus on the word "like." That word signifies God's desire for us to work towards perfection but understanding none can reach that apex in this world.

Let us explore obedience and it is meaning. To be obedient, is to do what is pleasing and acceptable to the Lord, and still acknowledges that we are sinners. I suppose giving thanks constantly for Jesus, and his blood that atones for our sin's past and present, creating a way for us to come to the Father. The gracious gift we receive as his children also opens the door to the same Father who keeps watch over everyone and recognizes the pursuit we are on. Let us not be so focused on our errors in the walk of our relationships. Let us be more prone to seeing the progress of our walk down the path. Therefore, stumbled but stand, make mistakes but not my fate, confess finds rest, and forgiving starts a way of living. Focus on the growth and the overcoming in and through your faith. People in whole, should forgive and forget the wrongs of our lives retaining and remembering the moments of miracles and fortitude of our faith. Sharing with the multitudes all the amazing things God has shown and done in us. The word says He remembers our trespasses not.

Finally, take this approach in your relationships. It is not possible to please everyone all the time. Learn to be patient, kind, and gentle through it all. Conduct yourself with humility and self-control and in turn, your relationships will be full of peace, love, and

Christian Section 2

HIS WELL DOTH NOT RUNNETH DRY

Tributes

RESTORATION & REFUGE

1. A WOMAN BLESSED BY THE WELL
2. MOTHER AND MY FATHER'S COMMANDMEN
3. UNLIKELY REFUGE

RESTORATION & REFUGE

Tributes

A moment we can take solace. Perhaps, a person able to offer sympathy, encouragement, or rest. Then again, it could be a place very dear to our hearts, few could believe possible, the racing thoughts dissipate, cleansing and letting go occurred in this haven of safety. Even a profound enlightenment and spiritual restoration. Two requirements are necessary to reach these destinations. Inner reflection and remembrance, that His grace is constantly enough when we are weak, He is made strong; therefore, bringing glory to His purpose and will. All the while, restoring what we lost of ourselves and in need of repair. His well never runs dry; we just forget to drink.

The Holy Spirit will intercede upon our behalf, when Gods children have found the lows, all things are at His mercy. Keeping with His promise, the spirit will use the fruits to replenish those in need of comfort. The three tributes in this section have a common trait. What is the link? Women and how they pertain to my story of battles with trust the female species. Moreover, believing one might be relationally present for their loved ones or spouse in need. The three tributes offered changed my thinking and perception.

A WOMAN BLESSED BY THE WELL

My life these past few years has begun to change in the way I view God's creation called woman. Please, before you skip this chapter, let me explain. Much of my experience came through living with the absence of stability at home. Constant re-locating not only by residence but the people who were deemed unlucky winners of my caretaking. This led to a severe lack of trust in women. I lived with my mom, great grandmother, and various aunts. The men would also frequently change which kept me from even attempting to create a bond with them. Why subject myself to the loss of more relationships? I am not saying that my family were all horrible people or parental figures. Just there was not any unity or trust that you could cling to with confidence.

I hope that my preceding insight helps to enlighten and allots the proper recognition of what wonderful and virtuous women I have encountered since being born again. God has blessed me with a new prism and hope I lacked for 30 plus years concerning trust when it pertained to God's most lovely creation. Slowly, my abandonment and trust issues have faded through vigorous testing and maturation. This is in large part to a few women of God that He put in my pathway to witness and be examples for me, sometimes, even oblivious to these ladies in doing so.

First, Carol, a courageous and dedicated mother and wife. She spends her time assisting the athletic dept. of schools in our community few could ever manage. The traveling, cooking, cleaning, counseling, and scheduling pipeline she steady offers to the kids and parents is a wonderful vision of the gift of service and sacrifice. However, all this is almost unbelievable when adding that her youngest child is battling a stubborn form of cancer at just 8 years old. She does not miss a beat or lose her positive demeanor. Instead, Carol's faith during this crisis seems to have increased when many might have collapsed with complete understanding from bystanders. Not Carol, this woman's courage and inspiring outlook on life remains intact and uplifting to all those crossing the path of her life's journey. Carol has helped me with my outlook and insecurities. More incredible, is without even directly dealing with me on any issues I fight. Her impact on my ability to believe not all people, quit, leave, or abandon sacred relationships is priceless. The improvement of my husbandry, fatherhood, and friendship reliance simply with her faith in God while completely unaware is humbling. God is magnificently healing old wounds through Carol's dedicated service and virtue from oblivion. I give God glory for His ways of using us for good in others' lives when we just stay the path.

I will close this out by offering an abundance of gratitude to the steadfast women of God out there who get weary at moments but will not surrender to the enemy. Those foolish tactics the devil attempts cannot stand against your faith. Please, remember that you are making a difference. Just because there is not a billboard or neon sign with your name on it here on earth for all your works and service, does not mean that your humility and faith engulfing your spirit will not decorate your crown in heaven. Much appreciation and a job well done faithful servant by the highest will be the greeting when your journey concludes.

MOTHER AND MY FATHER'S COMMANDMENT

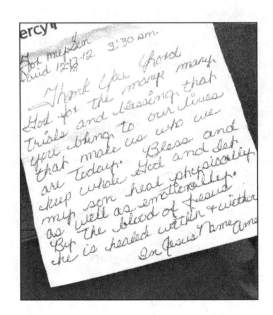

My mother and I did not have the best relationship. In fact, I only lived with her about three years of my childhood. Those ages were from 10 till 13 roughly. Mother was not mean just too busy chasing love and other things that were not good for her. In fact, she really did not know proper love in a Godly sense, ever. She married many times and had many miscarriages. Her love for me for a while was a bit inappropriate. Unfortunately, I had such a longing for her affection that I would take any attention offered. Even received from a belligerent state of confusion, which she would ask where she was and forget that I happen to be her adolescent boy, not Tom, Brian, or Bill.

For many years as an adult after moving out on my own at sixteen, I had little contact

D.R. Birch

with anyone in my family, let alone my mother. Sadly, my mother never even had the chance to meet my youngest daughter, Jordy. To put this in perspective, my mother died in 2016 and my daughter was 11 at the time. I could not deal with the abandonment nor the adulterated affection issues at the time.

However, I did see my mother following my divorce with the mother of my children. Divorce you say! Shocker, considering we never set forth one day in Gods house the entirety of the marriage and living together. That is another story though. I decided with not much holding me back to travel to the Midwest and see my mother who had been in poor health for quite a period. I cannot take credit for the idea to amend and forgive. Coercion from another person I was close friends with convinced me that it would be good for both of us to take a trip.

Arriving did not bring me to this amazing let go moment. I remained rigid and almost arrogant as I saw the modest place that she lived in with my nephew and sister. Of course, smoking and taking whatever, she could get the doctor to prescribe. By now I am sure some are reading this and asking how this fits anywhere behind Carol or within the promise. Well, God knows the hairs on our heads. He also knew that we would not have much time together nor Ideal in circumstance. Only days after arriving and becoming situated, I had a severe accident which left me virtually helpless to care for myself for months. Grief and guilt accompanied the physical damage. I lost like I had never experienced before and dealt with the emotional anguish that I will spare readers. As people checked in on me or wrote, my mother did not leave my side. Even in her weak and fragile condition, she would help clothe me and go to the bathroom. She held me at night when I had night terrors. We had many talks in that period. My mother began showing me in the hardest of circumstances, with death knocking, that she would not abandon me nor hurt me. I could trust her to be my mom.

We became close and had laughs but it was not to last. Due to my unavoidable circumstances that required resolution and her health which designated her to a hospice center. Ironically, my mom would die without my sister nor me accompanying and providing comfort of loved ones. All those years I felt unwanted and now here I am the guilty one of desertion. Amazingly, her sense of humor never decreased still joking about being famous for her shiny bald head instead of her singing abilities. The last letter she would write me while I paid my dues confirmed repentance, acceptance, forgiveness that shined bright of the promise.

No doubt, she became close with the father, as did I, both of us in a place of reflection and realization. See, the beauty in the tragedy is that the lord during are toughest trials and hardships can accomplish good. He gave me my mom and her a son full of forgiveness and fond memories, in the farewell. Most importantly, He brought us both into His family. We received salvation through the promise. Finally, I can attest to honoring my mother with these few words written in this book. In these words that align me with the Father's commandment to write the book. I give Him all the glory, thank you, Father.

People who are dealing with issues from childhood that need resolve please read this as many times as it takes to forgive the one you are holding in contempt.

God made this lesson transparent and with mirror imaging.

UNLIKELY REFUGE

The lord's word in Exodus talks of cities of refuge for those in need of time to heal wounds. Sometimes, it is difficult to understand and almost impossible to accept this truth because of the pain and loss some must endure. God, however, is no respecter of persons and even told pharaoh he would have compassion on whom, he would have compassion. Even stating, that He hated Esau. I am thankful for His loving grace He bestows on us as HIS children.

During my exile I would be given many opportunities to get closer to God and begin to feel the love and sacrifice Jesus made for us. My intimacy with God during this time still is so remarkable and humbling that brings merit to His, Saving Grace.

For now, let me tell you of this refuge. This dwelling place would allot me time to get educated in ministry and the word, gain certifications, and work on my body to give the lord a strong temple. Moreover, I learned how to help others become more sound and responsible adults. God literally slapped in my lap the chance to help less fortunate gain high school educations. In this strange but rewarding school setting I met many people from cultures that changed much of my preconceived notions. Although, none of them compared to a woman that was unmatched by whom I had the pleasure to know, thus far in life. Let me assure everyone that it was not a physical gravitation that captivated me. This is a lady that exuded dignity while glimmering with humility; a kind soul that still had the ability to draw respect out of her broad knowledge as an educator. These wonderful qualities pale in comparison, though, to her amazing love for the lord as she knew Him. God had blessed me with a friend and partner. Together we achieved much success in a less than desirable place. He had also opened my eyes to the image of what a Christian woman might appear to be. The Father's promise had reared again giving me in this place, a purpose, partnership, and the peace of the holy spirit which I shared everywhere I traveled within this community. It is been years since that time, but many faces remain an integral part of my life today. Including, close Christian brothers, mentors of the word, and my beloved and virtuous wife and best friend that the lord gifted me as a suitable helper who stood firm by my side during the storms. The lord showed me the way out of the wilderness. God had blessed me in an unlikely refuge with a complete restoration through cancelation of corrupt thinking and polluted lifestyle.

Christian Section 3

THE BETTER ROAD

Challenges

PEACEFUL PATHWAYS

1. WORSHIP WILD
2. TAG TEAM
3. S.I.M.P.L.E.

PEACEFUL PATHWAYS OF THE PROMISE

Challenges

The sooner we can start implementing this approach to memory, the road we travel will become much easier. Control issues are problematic for many. Then when you add that increased pressure of negative circumstances or unforeseen trials to the mix of your daily life, it becomes far worse. What is it about challenging times that makes a person want to have all control or say in the matter? This is when we really need to throw are hands up literally and start giving it to Jesus like he said to do. However, if you are anything like my wife or I, you tend to bang your head repeatedly against the wall that will not move (problems) until you are just about to fall out. Finally, relinquishing the power you thought you had residing in your flesh and allow the spirit to work and move mountains.

WORSHIP WILD

Worship according to me might differ for many as my conversion and coming to Christ came later in life. My brokenness that was born by being a knucklehead in most of my waking moments, presenting issues after my new identity. I know my salvation is secured but I cannot seem to get my feet out of the mud. I do not just step into sin, either I get lost in it. The point I am validating, is fretting on how a person worships or what they wear at the lord's house is not something God's concerned with at all. So, should we be concerned? God is concerned more so when we do not go to attend church. He does not receive glory when we withhold praise or worship to any degree. I tend to be the oddball when it comes to worship in my family.

My wife and I were in this very holy prayer room of her church. We both entered a room of adoration room loving and filled with the Spirit. Although, if one were monitoring from afar, they would see two diverse types of praise and worship completely in contrast. This situation caused me to reflect on other observations. I have fallen victim before from the judgments passed on according worship. In this room, my wife was sitting close to the alter and remained in utter silence through prayer. While she was quiet, I was feeling filled with the Spirit but acting fidgety and hyper in my actions. When the Spirit comes over me, sometimes I can appear a bit unorganized or radical. I assure you my senses are just stimulated by his Love and presence. Observing me you would find books and papers laid about and a sudden excitement to share insight with my wife. This urgency perturbed my wife's worship as on the fifth or sixth attempt to get her attention, she jerked her head about and shushed me like a child. I looked at her almost with dismay and without hesitation, replied, "Easy babe, we all do this reverence thing differently."

Think for a second, God would most assuredly get bored if there was only one type of reverence and worship. Some sit in stillness and sheer awe of God in His presence. This moment my wife carried this exact praise. This type of worship shows humility and respect for the Lord. That said, I am the kid from across the street and that is not how God designed me. I like to have multiple toys given by my Father in my sandbox. All the while, I am completely loving my Father during this time. The assurance of safety within my Father's house gives me that freedom of expression. Human fathers express a joy watching their children being happy and excited. How much more joy would it bring our Heavenly Father at seeing his children full of joy when being in His presence? Christians, conflict about what is appropriate in worship, attire, demeanor, songs, versus. Why?

My actions that night drove my wife crazy and in recognition, I applied politeness and reeled it in just a bit. Scripture came upon me and once again persisted to get her attention. That Scripture was Mt 18:3 when Jesus said, "Truly I tell you. Unless you change and become like children, you will never get into heaven." I do not know about you reader, but I do not see too many children in sheer awe and stillness when they go into the church.

My wife was not judging my style in this moment, irritation had stirred inside her from being disrupted of her praise. Wisdom would have all understand that praise and worship is beautiful music to God's ears despite era, style, or genre. Realistic evaluation gives clarity to the obvious, God created us and our gifts and abilities. Therefore, God finds joy in all music when giving glory to the father. We do not need another finite creature's approval in how we express our gratitude and thankfulness to the Father. Unconditionally He expresses love directly back towards us as he receives his glory. Sometimes you can even fill it engulf your entire body as the Spirit moves.

Sandbox or sitting room, reading, dancing, hollering like a little girl who won an award. All find favor when done with earnest desire to give glory to our God. When a passion is exhibited for Christ as a child performs for their parents, God receives glory and joy. I urge everyone critical of anyone's approach to the throne when offering praise and worship to end the judgement. Attempt to visualize worship with full attention and expression driven, like the love a child offers.

"Let's stop hazing and start praising." End OMEGA- judging and begin ALPHA-loving. Accomplishing this discipline, can graduate a person from defaulting honest analysis of ourselves, just to be a flaw finder in others.

Genuinely and Intimately,
Worshiping Wild!

TAG TEAM

You have just completed an extremely exhausting day at work. All you desire is taking a shower and relaxing with a movie. Possibly, vent a little to the wife and get some encouragement and nurturing of your own while portraying the pouty partner. However, your son, thirteen years of age seems extensively withdrawn, alarming a fatherly sense of something is up. Of course, being a parent, you are going to spark up conversation because parents are fixers. "What's the matter?", you ask. Suddenly, greeted with an issue not expected, bullying.

These are usually not too serious but can become severe when lingering on. Damage in various parts of your teen's mental, emotional, and spiritual states become threatened. A risk of physical affliction is possible too. The topic needs to be approached with the utmost awareness, kindness, gentleness, and self-control. The fruits of the spirit are necessary because of the child's sensitivity risk, if approached in a way that belittles the child or situation. The weight on your shoulders is to recognize the importance and handle this swiftly. In addition, allowing transparency with the significant counterpart of your demeanor and ability to proceed or halt because of a deficiency. If needed, pass the torch to your wife, and set a time to engage later about the matter including the other parent.

Proceed with all your heart as your Heavenly Father would you, bearing the fruit of the spirit and compassion and love of Jesus. Resolution and peace will be the result of this issue. Proceeding pre-maturely or half-heartedly could lead to anger, irrational advice, and emotional scars for the child and/or the parents. A family that's torn in battles born will become a family worn and the tears of the relationship quickly become shreds of relationship fabric that once kept all safe and warm from the outside world that wants to devour all good.

S.I.M.P.L.E.

The days are so hard when your reliance is on the flesh for contentment. Days when we allow this mindset to rule our current matters usually sets the course to a frequency of frustration followed by futile worldly attempts to repair. Lasting success is not achieved through the flesh. Why is this true?

People and the things of this world are not infinite nor are their characteristics of the flesh; however, the opposite is true of the Spirit. The trick is learning to search for your desires and needs that align with the spirit. Accomplishing this task takes vision and hearing. The spirit can be felt, occasionally. Our Spirit is only fed through the holy spirit and for that to take place we need a devotion to disciplined living for God. This takes skills of keen listening and mind's eye vision. Man cannot truly live on bread alone.

I remember a conversation with my wife that posed a question into how someone receives the spirit through others. This does occur but not true of every person, including Christians. Christians sin just like everyone else and when we commit sins, Christians, break a link in the chain that connects us to God's Spirit. Which leaves individuals, lacking fruit to repair spiritual wounds. Work to realize the self, monitor closely the spiritual walk. What is your personal faith meter read? This is crucial due to the flogging that occurs when a Christian succumbs to a sin that becomes a public announcement. Not one person can absolutely offer the Spirit through their body, mind, and soul, constantly. We all fall short, according to scripture. Therefore, leaving every individual who finds themselves in a crisis or ostracized by exposure of flaws, results in legalism and worldly conviction, instead of forgiveness and compassion from the church. Judgement of this nature, often, makes a member of the church turn and flee from their faith entirely. Christians need to awaken to the realization these moments are when God makes good on His promise and we need to have patience. The spirit intercedes and becomes real within the wretched soul or the prisoner considered, the worst of the worst. The love of Jesus lifts a person up from their lowest point. Then follows it by emotionally explaining the sacrifice He made for them, creating a humbled and contrite heart the spirit can use. Church take an inventory of the congregation and discern if this is happening where you attend services. If it is occurring, the gossip of the Godless, persecution of the prisoner, stoning the sinner, or flogging of your family, remember God created all things. Do not put God in a box according to human capabilities. Focus on yourself and pray for others, exuding and utilizing patience and self control. In doing so, one will have a chance to keep their tongue from lashing comments you will regret. Stepping away might be difficult if you deal with control issues. God's sovereignty over trials does not adhere to anyone's time schedule. Denying self, begins with looking in the mirror and focusing on that 2x4 wedged in your eye, this will take time to own it and remove. Repentance and confession of your own sin not others, ignites the spirit that can move mountains. This is how one can stand with their brethren entrapped by sin and magnify the glory for the lord.

Christian Section 4

WALKING THE ROAD

TALKING ABOUT WALKING

    1. IN BODY (Jesus Christ)
       SENSIBILITY of LOVE

    2. IN MIND (Father God)
       INTUITION of the STILL SMALL VOICE

    3. IN SPIRIT (Holy Spirit)
       FRUITS OF FREEDOM

TALKING ABOUT WALKING

Body, Mind and Spirit

"Knowledge is the knowing and Wisdom is the Application." This quote when fully lived out in our daily lives grants us the power to overcome and acceptance when we are overwhelmed. Walking the road with the lord takes commitment to stay connected to Christ in body, mind of God, and emotionally to the spirit. Walking this road is only possible by knowing the trinity intimately. Ready to face the little bumps or complete breakdowns along the road in front of you. The trinity assists through agape love, sovereign conscious and comforting support in your journey through this world and return home. By using the wisdom gained from the debris and dust storm left twisting behind you.

This section is a breakdown of the trinity from a broad scope. Although, it should suffice on bringing knowledge of proper alignment with the lord and insight to beginning to conduct and live righteous. Through biblical examples of the fruits of the spirit, and insight to your own sensibility concerning fellowship and how to experience love to its fullest potential. Also, listening to the sound of silence.

SENSIBILITY OF LOVE
JESUS CHRIST

Sensible love! Sounds like heaven, right? I mean, really, who would want the opposite love(irrational)? Irrational love is exhausting even downright maddening at times. Conflict in relationship is assured but does not succumb to shouting, belittling, breaking objects, and violence if it is a sensible love.

Sensible love, rather, appears in patience, kindness, and does not bathe in pride or lather up in envious attitudes. The bible even offers further definition in the love chapter, 13 of Corinthians. As wonderful of an example this is of love, we will wait to delve into it until later in the spirit section. I want to focus our attention on the senses God gave us to experience love in the fullness within the body.

The body has five senses. Those senses are sight, hearing, smell, taste, and touch. When the lord is moving in His temple (the body) we are given the capability to love sensible. This is what **SIGHT** might look like: Your eyes capable to lock in on each other and almost gaze into the soul of your mate. A spouse can conjure sensations with mere glances or gazes. We possess power from observation in mere seconds that our significant is needing comfort, fulfilling of desire, or encouragement. Examples might be a wanting of seconds on her delicious lasagna or reinforcement when the kids attempt to plot attacks to get their way. My wife can visually recognize defeatism in a slouching of one of my shoulders (I had no clue) or that I flap my arms slightly walking away. This sense is strong typically but also the easiest to obtain and retain **because** of memory, sense of the mind. Beware if this becomes a frequent fallback. The difference is true attentiveness to the moment and not seen out of an auto response from familiar history. An awareness tip of this happening is if you are multitasking frequently when engaged in contact or communication with your spouse. Please do not allow this to become the norm. When identified, pray for help in attentiveness to your partner. If not remedied this not only causes a great barrier in your relationship but removes God from the body. This can lead to a hardening of the heart as well. My wife and I have not encountered this issue. I believe our strength in this sense stems from an absence of seeing each other for many months during a group treatment expedition that I was House Elder and spokesman of for about forty men choosing a better road for themselves. Since returning our longing to see the other has remained intense. My wife daily has ability to grab my sight when she walks across the room.

My Beautiful Forever(wife), a new released movie in my life each waking day. She cannot breathe, moreover, move without alerting my **HEARING**: Do you know why God gave us two ears and one mouth? Where we have ability to hear twice as much as we say. What is more important is doing it wholeheartedly. Lackluster listeners are lame and low on love components, in those moments. Sure, sometimes it is mundane or not the bit interesting to you!

SONG OF SOLOMON 8:13

YOU WHO DWELLS IN THE GARDEN WITH FRIENDS IN ATTENDANCE, LET ME HEAR YOUR VOICE!

Hearing is not about you at least sometimes. We. Surprise cannot assist our partner with their concerns or needs with deaf lobes. Guess what else? We cannot receive the affirming messages we need either. That is what is so tricky about this sense. I know the voice of your spouse can clang like a cymbal; That voice can also be the sweetest music ever heard by you too. Unfortunately, a person cannot tune out or just turn off part of the audible connection. Sorry, selective hearing is not possible. Once you disconnect, you will soon realize how depleted and lost you have become. Take a little time and try and reflect on a point in your life when you were not receiving any words of encouragement or meaningful conversation. Perhaps, a time when nothing was being asked of you and nobody was calling for your opinion or advice. This is a low and lonely way to live. Not to mention this awful soundless studio of life leaves you deaf on God's direction for you as well. God speaks to us through others. We receive His peace through hearing.

Let us insert a new deductive thinking process to what you hear. Sometimes, as I make my way around the house, I sound like a bull in a china shop. Loud and irritating, by initial sound bite. Although, from a new deductive thinking process (DTP) one might hear the closing cabinet doors or tinging of dishes I fumble in the kitchen as sounds of enticement. Thinking deeper proves successful in my wife's listening gracefully, for these sounds bring favorites like Eggs Benedict served in bed. Made possible by my irritating early stirring. Done though with the intent of service and gratitude for my wife. If she happened to just yell or get angry prematurely then this act of service is negated and god's gift to her through the body is negated. Love is thwarted. I know there are readers saying give me that peace and quiet, forget the eggs. I know they say "Silence is Golden" but it can also be deafening to a relationship. Lose the ability to love through listening and communication and a sadness like none other will blanket you as you might see the love of your life but no longer really hear them. That is a silence born of hell not God's love. Confirmation of true hearing sensibility of love can be found in scriptures. So, let the sounds of your beloved be music to your ears, even if its awful music does not refrain from dancing to it.

Speaking of dancing, the **TOUCH** of love through the body. It is a foregone conclusion that a man loves to caress the cheek of his woman. A woman can get lost in the strength a man displays after mowing the lawn on a sweltering day or returning from the gym, glistening with perspiration that accentuates muscle definition. Subliminally, reminded of protection and safety when those arms are holding her. The yearnings of these attributes are ignited via sight in moments like this when the brain computes the picture. Activating, sense of touch with desire.

However, it is the subtle ways of touch that have immense ability to join a wife and husband as one flesh. Holding hands any random day displays affection and builds unity. Hands are remarkable executors of producing love with a touch. Some common examples: the shaking of hands that signify respect, trust, and even the closing of a deal in business. The playfulness delivered through petting, tickling, or even a hug that is intensified by the grip that starts with the hands that are wrapped around the other person.

Touch has power of faith produced in grips of a hug virtually able to heal a person, emotionally. Our very lord is manifested in a healing touch and one can feel His presence through prayer circles and the laying of hands. Jesus taught us faith is connected to the sense of touch with His own life experiences, i.e. the story of Lazarus and the girl who merely touched Jesus's cloak. Jesus told us, where two or more are gathered He would be present. That said, it is not possible truly to be in Jesus's presence and not be touched.

There is an intimacy in touch unlike the other senses of the body. Try not to fast forward your thoughts to sexual relations. Obviously, touch is a vital sense in the act of love making. This coming together of two which are considered one in the eyes of God is part of all the senses of love.

One last insight please heed, by chance the realization hits you that one sense is missing during these intimate moments, please communicate with your partner and pray to bring Jesus into the relationship. That way touch can reimplement the missing sense before the devil has an opportunity to attack where your relationship is currently weak.

Here is an image to lead us into a mindset on the sense of taste. Would Tarzan, if a sofa existed in the jungle, miss the opportunity to cuddle Jane upon it? I think not, nor should we, when allotted the time to soften and be close. He would, I imagine feed her berries and jane would reciprocate.

This opens the sense of **TASTE**, simply beginning with what our spouse finds tasty or appealing. Sharing in this shows trust, companionship, and interest in what the other finds appealing to this sense. The sharing of food and eating a meal together has been a staple in all cultures and all eras of existence of man. I am aware, personally, of the lost art of dinner as a family or couple at home these days. Life has become unmanageable with our obligations and the sacrifice of time with family has a taken a direct hit. I am guessing that I might be questioned why food tends to be so important. I assure you that manna is vital even in the bible we see the feeding of the 5000 and the last supper as key feasts that brought a closeness and faith and love few other instances could compare. This table offers much more than food. The taste of the lord within the body leaves a person quenched of thirst as well as fed. Loneliness loses a grip and love can be restored through the hope of unity. A final example I will offer is the Salvation Army and their free meal lines or maybe even your church partakes in this type of service. This act of tasteful generosity can heal, conquer, grow, mature, and replenish what is lost through the taste of sensibility. Through the masses or just a husband and wife when the lord is at the head of the table. "Love isn't an emotion, it's the union of two souls led by the lord, who is love, to intertwine and become one." If you have not realized it is not just about food but the tongue and what you decide or inadvertently serve your spouse that can destroy a relationship. Solomon put it simply,

PROVERBS 18:21

THE TONGUE HAS THE POWER OF LIFE AND DEATH AND THOSE WHO LOVE IT WILL EAT ITS FRUIT.

Finally, the sense of **SMELL** and how Jesus can bless us through nature and not always our favorite items or things. I should not waste time on the easy to please aromas of life. I am going to fill your sense with those dirty socks, gassy bathrooms, or filthy garages attached to and perpetrating us, offensively by our closest people. Yes, my wife and I have our own, less than pleasant gifts we share. These can become very irritating in moments of weakness encountered by the undesirables. Nevertheless, she is my PEACH! Some have the apple of their eye and to that I say, different fruit for different folks. Checkout Jesus's fruit tree in Galatians, which is one amazing fruit tree. To which He shares the love and emotion of Himself with us.

What I am trying to convey is the absence of the irritants mean we miss what is precious and lose what seems unreplaceable. Losing those precious fruits is not even a notion Christians would consider.

That suitable helper in Psalms 129:14 is Wonderfully and Fearfully made.

Therefore, it is perfect for you and part of how Jesus plans to show love to us through them. So, I encourage you not to disgrace those unpleasantries. Rather, engrave the less than scents deriving from your loved one to memory. I had a close friend I loved and knew for years that had this perfume that literally, made my nose so angry that my nostrils would flare, comparable to a bull seeing red. I would make every excuse to get away from her when she made the awful decision to wear this disturbance to the atmosphere. If she was visiting my apartment, I would make excuses that my apartment was stuffy and spray air freshener everywhere to drown the animal carcass perfume out(I now know the reason the French label perfume (EU de Toilette) . That is where this belonged, the toilet.

Unexpectedly, my friend lost her life tragedy way too early. This accident also had a major impact on me emotionally, and the trajectory of my life. I had the arduous task of going through her things including, clothing. As I filtered through the closets of her bedroom, I found a jersey of mine. She had confiscated it from me years earlier to have it to sleep in and because it had my scent on it. This all came flooding my mind when I picked that Dolphin jersey up out of the closet floor. Her perfume and scent slammed my senses. However, it was not obtrusive this time. I felt her presence through that strong smell which initiated such raw emotion, I sat and cried for a long time.

Jesus fed my yearning and need through that jersey. Totally unaware Jesus had started the healing with that scent that produced my first chance to mourn. Later, the lord gave me a revelation of wisdom that every scent that crosses the nose hairs(literally), can bless and assist us in keeping a loved person vivid long after their gone. The scent eventually faded from that jersey but not before the lord used it as a tool of coping that helped me begin a grieving needed to move through an awful and grim period of my life. Today, I do not take it for granted the evening kisses of my wife that resonate of a fruity and dry wine (I am not a fan, personally), among many other scents of bliss and unpleasantries. I implore all who read this book to meditate and breathe in this suggestion: Recall to memory, the fragrances of your family and ones dear to your heart, for it has ability that springs forth living moments of the departed for us through Jesus and the sensibility of love. Teach yourself through patience to enjoy it all, because in the end, it is all pleasantries.

THE MIND
FATHER GOD

That amazing still small voice that comes through clear, then other moments, seem to be a fleeting whisper lost in translation. Either way that voice is always audible and speaking to us with the best intent for our lives. That voice is always stirring and will continue to carry guidance for our lives.

The delivery as I said before differs. One might feel it in their gut almost to a nauseated state that is regurgitating a resounding DON'T TREAD THAT WAY! In contrast, a person might feel the urgency to lend a hand to someone or even rush into a burning building to save another life from the literal flame that destroys. That feat just might take the saved from the building crumbling to a mansion that is lit by the eternal flame of the Holy Spirit. We cannot be detoured from the calling upon our lives by God to do the deed that aligns with His will. Even as it might call for the ultimate sacrifice (your own). "There isn't a greater love than to lay down one's life for another. "These are the extremes, obviously. Still, I urge all of you to meditate on every moment that has a pause in it. A kind of a Selah that takes place in Psalms. This is when the spirit is interceding in your routine. In a sense, you have been called directly to listen for your own good or someone else's.

God is not just speaking in these moments to you but all the ones that fall in between, as well. Conversations that will heal you emotionally from grief and loss. Words of affirmation to believe in what you might have been offered like a promotion or opportunity to lead a group at church. The encouragement or courage to have difficult discussions with a dr. or a spouse and children. We are filled through the Holy spirit and God gives us the knowledge and wisdom to achieve it. The still small voice is the navigator of our steps, as it says in proverbs. We can choose the road to take but God has hold of the steering wheel.

I believe that we can hear easier the voice of our God, by being steadfast in prayer. Additionally, just with conversating with Him throughout the day. Granted, if you are not custom to doing this it might seem strange at first, but that strangeness will be put to rest when you are affirmed with His love and guidance. Lastly, but most importantly, that still small voice will not lead us to do evil things or, speak a pass, for us to commit sin. This would be the counterpart and the fallen angel deceiving us. Courageous acts, yes, one might be called to do, however, never a lewd or immoral work will be asked of us.

HOLY SPIRIT
PEACE, LOVE, JOY, & FAITH

PEACE

> ### PROVERBS 6:2-3
> "IF YOU'VE BEEN TRAPPED BY WHAT YOU SAID, OR ENSNARED BY THE WORDS OF YOUR MOUTH, THEN DO THIS, MY SON, GO AND HUMBLE YOURSELF."

RESET

We have all been at the brink of an argument that we wandered so far off the point we forgot the plot of this argument. At this junction, one or both individuals should have enough love for their mate to reset. The Lord tells us in Proverbs to stop quarreling as soon as it starts Proverbs 6:2-3. This works well we need to humble ourselves and swallow our pride during an argument with anyone, and seek resolve, it is foolish pride that builds us up and brings forth that anger and desire to prove validity of our points.

The evil that exist in the world through the enemy of all good strives and feeds off this irrational behavior. He despises love and kindness, gentleness and faithfulness, peace, and patience, and yes even joy and goodness. All of us have made comments that we wish we could rescind. That is what reset is all about. A call word if you will, given us by the Lord our wonderful counselor. Here we are forced to humble and assertively focus on something positive we hold true of the other individual we are engaged with in conflict. Sure, your mind will have trouble letting go of the thought that is chewing on your patience like some rabid dog out of a movie. Do not fret, revisiting the topic is open to do so, once calm. Also, after prayer,

Let me offer this little bit of information nothing in this world works to deviate you from conflict more than prayer. This frustrates the enemy because once you bring the Holy Spirit into the equation he cannot enter. So, I encourage anyone who is a believer that if you find yourself in the beginning stages of conflict. I.e. tension in your shoulders, tightening of the jaw, watery eyes, clenched fist, pacing, and ultimately using words to hurt or worse. Please by all means conjure the strength to ask your partner humbly to pray with you.

Even a boxer takes a minute between rounds to compose themselves and rest i.e. drinking water, getting a massage, and direction for the next round of conflict. He is the peace that makes the two of us one in our union. He is the dividing wall that separates our love from being invaded by hostility. When we accept Him into our lives, we are one with Him through the blood of his precious son. Therefore, I say pray and in doing so, I promise you will begin to feel calmer and see the anger begin to subside right from your partners face.

Prayer is one of the building blocks of a solid relationship. It is where two people let go of their pride and control to submit to something greater than anything else, God's comforter. We must remember if we allow ourselves to breach the walls of our significant other with harsh comments, we are allowing ourselves to be controlled by evil. The good word states, the hardest part of the body to control is the tongue. Stay aware of yourself do not allow it to lash out like a whip and hurt the ones you love the most. Reset yourself like an alarm clock, hit the snooze button already. Practicing some type of clause with a word like reset will build a habitual haven with Gods guiding light and prayer. In closing, I would like to remind all people in relationships that the person you married is not your opponent. That person standing in front of you is a component of your own self. Therefore, allow yourself time to breathe and rationalize the situation. Be calculated and mindful of how you speak and respond while listening to your partner. A boxer is calculated and does not lose control inside the ring. In fact, does not it almost seem as if it is not even that big of a deal that they are getting punch to death. It is called self-control; this is one of the Lords fruits very precious for those who have it. Reset it and get it

FAITH

> ## JAMES 1:2-3
>
> COUNT IT PURE JOY, MY BROTHERS, WHEN YOU FACE MANY TRIALS OF MANY KINDS. BECAUSE YOU KNOW THAT THE TESTING OF YOUR FAITH DEVELOPS PERSEVERANCE.

Remembering that we are his children and our whole existence is based on it, as a well the reason for the journey. TAKE COMFORT IN ANY CIRCUMSTANCE OR STRUGGLE, THAT THE PROMISE IS TRUE! Despite how hard the obstacle or how many come against you because of your mistakes. It will all work for the good in the end for those like you, believer.

JOY

> ## ISAIAH 61:7
>
> INSTEAD OF THEIR SHARE MY PEOPLE WILL RECEIVE A DOUBLE PORTION, AND INSTEAD OF DISGRACE THEY WILL REJOICE IN THEIR INHERITANCE; AND THEY WILL RECEIVE A DOUBLE PORTION IN THEIR LAND AND EVERLASTING JOY WILL BE THEIRS.

In context of today, shame and disgrace are not a stranger to any of us. Broken marriages, falling short on commitments, succumbing to temptations, and the list goes on. Our spouse, friends, co-workers, kids, and even strangers can impose these harsh sentiments. This overwhelming attack can have us reeling. We forget though, if from man we should remain steadfast. If we are doing God's work or, at least, in line through obedient living we need not be concerned. Use discernment concerning the decisions you have made. Utilize scripture to reaffirm your stance. I assure you these trials you face will result in the pure joy of what God promises those in line with His will. This promise is also double portioned here on this earth as in eternity.

LOVE

1ST CORINTHIANS 13:7

LOVE ALWAYS PROTECTS, ALWAYS TRUSTS, ALWAYS HOPES, ALWAYS PERSEVERES.

The love chapter as it is commonly referred to. This is the model that God made. An agape love, no doubt. To be the downer, none of us can achieve this type of love constantly. That is why the word ALWAYS has been incorporated, I think. This gives an objective or prototype of our action not success in the spirit. When we fail, we must not quit, it is a matter of Always striving.

That said, lets breakdown this verse. First, protection of your loved ones. Warning, this does not mean obsessiveness or control. All humans have free will awarded by God to humanity. For example, mt teenage daughter decides for herself where to hang out and with whom she likes, for the most part. I must allow her to make poor decisions as well. God works in the mud of our sin and mistakes, maturing us along the way. Protection can be identified in guidance, not at all control over another, and boundaries instead of obsession.

Next is trust which also relates to free will. This time let us use a spouse and the concern of her heart and its truth. Trust that if your relationship has the almighty at the center your bond can withstand the temptation. Despite whatever the concern or circumstance.

The hope of love is the manifestation of you and your spouse's dreams and goals that align with God's will. Hope shows up with faith by its side, and a way of implementing and growing that mustard seed, is prayer together.

Finally, persevere through everything that comes your way. Knowing that in doing this you will receive more faith and hope in your marriage. Always anticipating the storm to dissipate. Never quit on your spouse or kids. We are conquers made possible of victory in Jesus. So, confront the adversary and rage into the battlefield prepared and protected by the armor of God. In doing so, the relationship will blossom like a flower in spring with each new day and glory given to God. We can overcome the failures of our relationships because the price has been paid for all sin, past or present.

D.R. Birch

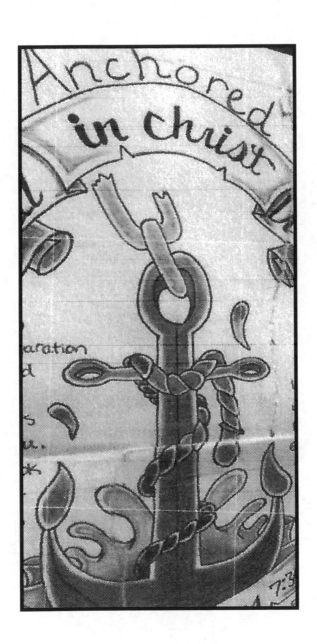

Center of Creation

MOMENTS

- W/ THE HIGHLY EXALTED
- NEMESIS
- KNOWLEDGE and WISDOM
- SILENT CONVICTION
- WITNESSING CHRIST
- REVELATION
- DIVINE DESIGN

THE HIGHLY EXALTED

True encounters with our Father right here on earth that left me in awe and deeper in love with my savior. I hope that these memories I share which are precious to me and solidify the faithful assurance in me. I pray these moments bring reminders of your own experiences to mind and encourage you to share those testimonies. Not because we are called to but to create a thirst for a relationship like yours too in others. All the while shattering that sometimes present awkwardness we feel when sharing. You know, we start to wonder, if the listener might think we are crazy or something. Well guess what we are, CRAZY in love and on fire for God. Some believe, the only way to keep it is to give it away, and here are a few of mine:

KNOWLEDGE AND WISDOM

This one really touches me personally. My wife and I spent a lot of time apart during the early years of our relationship. Not because we chose for it to be this way, but circumstances just did not permit. In addition to this I believe God ordained it. There was a lot my wife and I had to come to terms within our own lives. This is not to say we are not in contact through conversation. Daily, we interacted and did our part to encourage and express our devotion and affection. Still at this point, we were not married, we also had not been sexually active with each other. We had carnal needs and temptations and we had opportunities during a few visits but refrained and kept our self-control. I divulged this information to clarify how important it is to build the relationship, spiritually first. See this was and is the most vital part of our relationship. In the beginning, we had rocky times with our personality clashes and old habits from past relationships. Nevertheless, the one that ignited our attention in discovering more about one another is our common love and interest in God. This character and desire of our heart to please God is without a doubt what hold us together. The saying in the scripture: By wisdom, a house is built. Wisdom is God. The all-knowing-omniscient and through understanding, its established meaning that with God at the center of your family your roots will be established firmly with understanding where to get instruction when problems arise. Finally, your rooms are filled with treasure through knowledge. Knowledge that is obtained through understanding that your answers lie in God's wisdom to see you through the trials and maintain the structure of which is our family with love, encouragement, and obedience.

NEMISIS

Anyone who knows my name is privy of my dislike and fear of birds. This comes with just cause because of traumatic experiences in my adolescent years. These attacks include a frightening attempt by a murder of ravens at retrieving break from a snow christened field. Apparently bread and other delights were in the field for the taking. Unfortunately, so was I as I headed home in a hurry after school to beat the snowstorm. To my surprise, I had entered the diving point, of the murder and my clothing seemed inviting like the field. This was obvious as particles of my sweater were being torn from me and accompanied with this assault was the picking of my curly-hair I had way back when that I assume now screamed NEST. Of course, I got free of the violence and realized never was I to be a like the devil spawn.

There were two other encounters of severity concerning birds in early adulthood.

First, a fist fight with an emu. This happened at a costume party in which I made my way outside to the yard and had begun to lean on a fence. This fence was also part of an open topped chicken run that had a crazy emu. Apparently threatened by my less than masculine costume and invasion of his coop, this bird made way to face me after a few trips up and down the fence line squawking and dancing about. Reminded me of a WWE wrestler. Finally, Emu the Great face off with me and took a bob at my beverage. Missing the drink and shocking me all the same, I realized as I yelled at my buddy to look at this bird. That he was no playing with me; he was kicking the fence as well. Thanks be to God the fence did not give way like my pride or more than my pride would have ended broken. Pride had me with an audience take a few swings at the emu. Missing all but once when I grazed a punch to the throat. With each swig he would peck my elbows and ultimately spill my drink and make me fall with a haymaker missing badly. To which he kicked up some dust from the ground on me and ran away. Laughs at the epic loss to Emu the Great still did not stop.

The other involved more Ravens which ended with me at the hospital in Anaphylactic shock. I deserved it; I suppose. This was a hunting accident of horrific consequences.

Fast forward to my days after becoming a Christian and still in my exile stages, I spent many days of meditation and conversation out on a distant part of complex acreage. I enjoyed the stillness and had been in search of answers concerning my future. My mother had recently died, and I had not really had any contact with loved ones in a while. Anxiety was high and I sat alone. A chilly day in the fall which had a breeze I can still feel in thought. Few people were about and not a soul on the farm I looked upon as I sit on a curb. Praying quietly, I began to feel very lonely and unvalued by my family. Kinship relatives are whom I am speaking about mainly.

In the trees on the edge of the farm with very few leaves, were a host of sparrows not affected by the chill of the wind, I suppose. The sparrow song was not moving me in an effective way, especially since I had begun to sob quietly. I could feel my lonely sadness turning to a bit of annoyance with a hint of anger. As I reached a limit to the sparrows chirps and song, I threw a couple of pebbles their direction. Standing up with tears in my eyes to gather myself and head back to the bay house, all went quiet. I looked about because the sounds of the sparrows went to quietly so quickly, that it was eerie. No birdsong, no intercom, missing was the bounce of a ball or useless chatter. What did remain was a sparrow all alone standing at my feet. He looked up at me with the little head cocked to the side. Comparable to a dog's expression when his master speaks to him/her. I had for a second thought, to go on as I did not want to be seen crying. Still this sparrow had an ominous demeanor towards me that kept me captive. Almost like he knew my anguish and wanted to comfort me. As I was making my way back to the curb, I looked up and saw that the sparrow had followed me. At first, I simply had lost any ability to focus on anything other than this little bird. Fearless it stood and walked periodically in front of me. Strangely enough, never pecking for food. Two other interesting facts about little sparrow is his focus stayed on me and he had no apparent injuries. Sparrow sat with me for about ten minutes and the peace I felt during has been superior to almost any other experience. Sitting with the creature, I received reaffirming messages that seemed conveyed to me and not created by my burdened mind. Before Sparrow, all my thoughts were gloomy. Now they were full of love and rest. This brought me comfort that had to come from the comforter and the wonderful counselor. The Holy Spirit had brought forth a visual way to relieve me of lonely thoughts and overwhelming grief that had haunted me frequently in those years.

Sweet Holy Spirit, thank you so much for the powerful and soothing nature of your dwelling. This moment will forever be embedded in my mind and touch my soul with every moment spent in retrospect of the Sparrow. I pray other speak of these wonders of love that occurred in their lives. That day I lacked the strength to escape the cloud of gloom. I did not possess the faith to move the mountain out of my way. Hope was headed for less. Then you came to me in sensible love fashion and rescued me. Restoring all that had been depleted and filled my heart with a warmth that lasted days. I felt as if I received the best gift or present ever. Thank you for showing me the attentiveness I lacked. I give all glory for the clever way you had me hear your song of love for me. Restoring my hope with an opportunity to touch one of God's creations that I would have never touched not fifteen minutes before. Finally, the sweet taste and touch of the autumn through the breeze, birds, and landscape which remains as a portrait of my heart.

SILENT CONVICTION

During a men's treatment excursion dealing with character flaws and fears. I had the pleasure of attending church sessions voluntarily hosted by various denominations of Christianity and a wonderful opportunity to gain new friends along with gaining a mentor.

One evening prior to services I was headed to the shower and roll call to attend had started. Frustration and an indecisiveness rose within me because I still needed to finish a letter and make a call to Jill which I would miss if I went to service. Nevertheless, I could not resist the spirit's conviction. So, I went late and finished the letter first. Then as I went to the mailbox, I could hear worship had started. Stirring more procrastination to consume me, as I returned to loft on the fifth to convince someone to go with me. To no avail, I was left to attend alone without comrades. At this point I begin to believe and see that God was testing me.

I arrived fashionably late missing the praise and worship but caught the last 10 minutes of a sermon on the great white throne judgement. I made my peace that this is the message I needed to hear. Upon leaving, I approached a man of about 75 handing out materials. I later heard he had throat disease, but not before he reached for me and grabbed my hand sternly and started to mumble inaudible sounds. Meanwhile, shaking his arthritic appearing finger as if scolding me. This was further convincing as his aged eyed glared with a "how dare you," stare. The message God had for me was delivered at that moment, "you fool, get your act together".

The impact of conviction felt there for my selfishness was my great white throne judgement. My fleshly desire attempting to overthrow my time to praise my father was shameful and. The intensity of this man who did not have a voice to sing or worship God, as I stood well equipped with to bring praise that day, still thunders of God's love like none other, I have ever heard.

WITNESSING CHRIST

CORONA CRISIS

Once again Carol (WOMAN AT THE WELL) displayed remarkable fruit and resolve in who she is in Christ Jesus. She was awarded a trip to Disney world for the bravery of the whole family, especially, Little Dale in his battle with a disease. Graciously, accepting the gift of shocking opportunity, otherwise unlikely. The family Embarked upon the vacation. Which occurred early during the crisis. Denying her son some much needed time to be a kid was not going to happen.

After the arrival back home from Florida, Carol went to the doctor, and heard the diagnosis of Coronavirus that thrusted a guilt and collapsing fear atop being infected. The priority was to quarantine but knew the family needed testing and social distancing as well. The emotional weight concerning her immune compromised child in harms way had to be awful attempting to cope, faithfully and not get angry.

However, the lord had other plans. The end of testing proved Carol to be the only one in her family that contracted the virus. That relief led Carol to isolate herself solely to her bedroom for 15 days or so. Carol did not stop with safety of her family, she decided not to hide in confinement; Instead, defying the virus by sharing her information of not only being infected but the first in our community. The humbling disclosure of her condition was executed to protect others, not for empathy. I am in awe of the honest determination to face her battles and do what is right and never quit, leave, or abandon the purpose at hand or the people around her.

REVELATIONS

- *ABSENCE OF SOMEONE DOES NOT MEAN ABANDONMENT, ALL ACCOUNTS.*
- *UNAWARE OF YOUR NEEDS DOES NOT TRANSLATE TO CARING LESS ABOUT YOU.*
- *A PERSON MISSING FROM YOUR LIFE IS NOT DEFINITIVE NEGLECT.*
- *LONELY IS NOT THE SAME AS ALONE.*
- *LONELY DEFINES AS: SELFISHLY LOST IN ONE'S PITY.*
- *ALONE ONLY TRULY EXISTS IF SOMEBODY IS VOID OF THE HOLY SPIRIT.*

*These are in revelation to the **Mother and Father's Commandment**. I learned by the end of my mother's time here on earth, that the feelings I had as a child of neglect or loneliness were and are still real for many. However, this does not conclude, evidence of how the other person feels or desires to subject the lonely individual with regularly. I am thankful to the lord for my small window of time with my mom to learn these facts. In turn, the forgiveness given by both her and I brought God's peace and understanding. Folks, if there are any of you out there from broken homes or missing parents carrying weight of guilt or hurt from when you were a child, please, at least here the person out and allow yourself an opportunity for resolution before it's too late. It was all worth for me despite the awful child upbringing and tragic way my life had brought my mother and I face to face again.*

DIVINE DESIGN

Four years minus forty days
Duration of my refining
Extensive molding for the designing
Of shattered clay.
        Today I walk better roads with,
Amazing Grace.
        Down pathways not broken,
As a new creation.
        Blessed to find love above
And a wife by my side.
        The old me, a memory
My Journey alive in being born again.
AND ALL HIS CHILDREN RAISE, PRAISE, & SAY AMEN.

FINAL WORD FOR THE SKEPTIC

AN EXTRAORDINARY RELATIONSHIP AWAITS YOU. ONE WITH A LOVE SO PURE AND STRONG, IT'S CAPABLE OF EMPOWERING YOU TO IMPACT OTHERS IN ALL REQUISITES OF RELATIONSHIPS. TRUE JOY IS FOUND IN THE COMPANY OF OTHERS THAT HAVE A BOND OF PEACE WITH YOU. ALLOWING AN OPENESS AMONG PEOPLE CLOSE TO YOU THAT CREATES CONNECTIONS BUILT ON TRUST, RESPECT, AND SACRIFICE. THIS WILL REQUIRE A SPIRTUAL LIFE PRESERVER AND AN UPLIFTING ENDLESS FAITH. I'LL SUM IT UP FOR YOU WITH ONE WORD, SALVATION! May god draw you near and start His finishing work in you where you can abound in His amazing grace. AMEN.

Skeptic Section 4

MODERN DAY

Apostles do much work abroad and with many, often in strange lands. The impact of these gifts take much sacrifice and lots of encouragement for the flock that's astray or missing the ability or opportunity of the gospel.

Evangelists are equipped with ability to convince and protect the flock from attack by educating Christians of measures and tools to do the same for their immediate families. In addition, to this evangelist grow the herd with the word.

Prophets possess capabilities to pierce through the fog of foe and fear sent at us to fool us by the devil to knock us from the path. This comes from using spiritual hearing and vision which is directly connected to gods knowledge and wisdom. This is recognized and brought to the congregation's reality through faith. The evidence is in the unseen and things hoped for that produces miracles for believers and builds a churches foundation correctly.

ADMINISTRATION – maintains a central focus.

LEADERSHIP – navigates the congregation.

TEACHING – maturation in the word.

KNOWLEDGE – trainer of word of God.

WISDOM – of the people and their works.

PROPHECY – with ability that leads people to conviction of sin.

DISCERNMENT – investigator of character and true intent.

EXHORTATION – counselor of encouragement.

FAITH – believer with supernatural trust in God.

EVANGELISM – able to bring others to God.

APOSTLESHIP – missionary of word abroad.

SERVICE – servant of humility, assist many in small fashion.

MERCY – empathizer and cheerfully compassionate towards others.

GIVING – exhibits and spreads joy freely in giving.

HOSPITALITY – host to all comers with special ability to ease anxiety with presence.

THE LORD PROVIDES THROUGH YOUR GIFTS TO THOSE IN NEED AND IN THE PROCESS MAINTAINS HIS PROMISE TO US ALL.

BODY
WORKS OF THE SPIRIT

This is a list of gifts that I see broken down into three categories head-shipped by 3 gifts all in their own. I hope this list will intrigue the reader to do a spiritual gifts survey, perhaps. Possibly opening a better definition on your strongest attributes and where you can make a difference. In addition, to an outward praise and glory for our Father for this gift and enlightening thereof . These surveys can be found online by various organizations and websites of Christianity.

These gifts of the spirit are manifested through the works you commit, relationships entered, and services offered by you while led and indwelled by the holy spirit. The lists are as follows:

APOSTLESHIP	EVANGELISM	PROPHECY
Giving	**Administration**	**Knowledge**
Hospitality	**Mercy**	**Discernment**
Exhortation	**Teaching**	**Wisdom**
Service	**Leadership**	**Faith**

BODY
WORKS OF THE SPIRIT

The spirit uses the body to produce the will of God through the service of the faith and for others. We all have at least one spiritual gift. Many are already anxious to know the list. Well, I am going to give it to you with a form of basic overview. I encourage everyone to do an extensive questionnaire that evaluates and scores the different gifts. Then you will be a step further in knowing how God made you and possibly the direction in life you should go. In doing so, you will realize an objective and the tool God gifted you in the world.

HINT: The gift will feel easy and bring you a sense of peace or joy or both.

This is a list moreover, than a story or an account. I hope this list will intrigue at least curiosity to do a spiritual gifts survey that will define your strong and weak points. You will find the top three fit your persona quite perfectly, so long, as you answer the questions honestly and not out of desire or aspiration.

These gifts of the spirit or manifested through the works you commit, relationships entered, and services offered displaying the fruits of the character of holy spirit. So, the list as Paul attests:

MIND
INFECTED, EFFECTED

> ### PROVERBS 16:25
> STATES DILEMMA THE BEST: THERE IS A WAY THAT SEEMS RIGHT TO A MAN BUT IN THE END, IT LEADS TO DEATH.

HARDNESS OF THE HEART

When dealing with the heart as a worldly soul or skeptic, perhaps. This is an issue of the mind through worldly ways that suppresses the true flesh of the heart. Hardness is what the enemy of yourself desires. When of the world one might see the boundaries or the guarding of opening up as a security fence keeping you from relational pain and awful scars of your life rising upon in memory causing almost a reenactment of living it all over. This might be true to an extent, but this approach also prohibits healing of the wounds and little chance of building relationships the right way. One must face the pain and fear of another heartbreak to find the bliss and fulfillment of a companion. Furthermore, receiving God into your life and His salvation and Grace.

To better understand what the previous paragraph alludes to, we must dive into the broad Biblical meaning of heart. The Bible says the heart is the center of the human personality producing things that typically would be ascribed cognitively. Scripture informs us that a slew of emotions and feelings from grief to joy are produced through the heart. Meditating upon that one should see it easy how a hardened heart might numb an individual's conceptualization and perception with relationships. Faithful Christians are not immune to this any more or less than the sceptic. Many a people from scripture dealt with hardened hearts. For example, the Israelites and their wondering through the wilderness. They showed truly little faith, just like the disciples at times refused Jesus's assurance that He would take care of all their needs if they would seek His kingdom first.

The culprit to hardening of heart is none other than sin. Doing what is wrong when you should be doing what is right. Furthermore, when it is repeated continuously to the point of being consumed by it. A person will grow immune to the conviction of doing what is wrong during this process. We begin to tune out that still-small voice of conscious which is none other than Yahweh himself. As we continue to engage in these immoral acts of debauchery and worldly living, we begin to suffocate love's ability to live inside us. Pride is another cause that can stone wall your heart. In a sense, pride is a God complex. One begins to believe only in themselves and that they have all the answers. A person's absent-mindedness of a power greater than themselves is a loss of humility and will surely take the person down a road of destruction. Typically declared through the blame game upon others and even God himself, one loses the ability to confess their shortcomings and faults and in turn losing the ability to be forgiven. Revelation after revelation came for me showing me why so many mistakes were repeated in my life and why tragedy struck with loss of life, friendships, and self as I knew me to be. Thankfully, it does not take everyone as long as it did me to receive a way of thinking and lose their heart of stone.

Proverbs 16:25 states dilemma the best: There is a way that seems right to a man but in the end, it leads to death. The anecdote is simply confession and walking through past hurts, griefs, and accepting the truth that you cannot do "it" alone. That truly in the end you are not in control and be ok with that. When you confess these failures, God comes to our side and relieves us of our anguish which was keeping our hearts from letting go. However, be aware that this will not be a quick fix. After repenting of your sins, you can continue down the path of releasing all your failures and hurts by studying God's words.

Do not let this last bit of information discourage you because even faithful Christians suffer setbacks, disappointments, and suffer trials within their lives. The Lord tells us to rejoice through the struggles because there is a maturation of our being that brings us closer to Christ. In that struggle we continue to let go and just Let GOD. Practicing that humility. The world's richest are no comparison to God's love.

D.R. Birch

KINDNESS

COLOSSIANS 1:17

HE IS BEFORE ALL THINGS, AND IN HIM ALL THINGS HOLD TOGETHER.

TIMELESS

Time is the most valuable commodity we as humans have at our disposal. Unfortunately, that is just what we do with it. Throw it down the proverbial garbage disposal. Sure, we accomplish great tasks and utilize time to the best of its ability to meet the needs of appointments and job duties, education ambitions and necessities, we organize and rearrange dates, times, events to mee the busy schedule of our modern fast lane lives. To the basic eye of the public or even yourselves, you might appear to be the best game manager time has ever encountered. However, what we fail to see is the lack of attention needed by our loved ones. Our relationship and our children are at the core of why we juggle our lifestyles like we are an act in the circus. Why do we decide to operate like we do not have a minute to spare? Because we feel the need to provide for our families. Nevertheless, this approach to life leaves us severely thirsty for fulfillment in many requisites.

We must not forget to include being a part of our loved one's life. Your spouse needs physical and intimate interaction and so do the kids. If we drive ourselves to the point of shear exhaustion every day, we deprive everyone including yourself of the fuel that got everything started in this family in the first place. We must keep contact with our wives and children, we must not forget to be involved intimately through conversation and loving care. Allow time to listen to their day and activities. Be alert and available to their inner concerns. Do not sacrifice the love, joy, kindness, ang gentleness of your relationships just for provisions. All of these were fulfilled prior to the providing and managing. These are the qualities all people truly need and deserve.

Spiritually we need to spend time with God and continue to grow as a believer and as a unit. Without the component of God all things fall apart. Colossians 1:17 confirms this

He is before all things and in Him all things hold together. I realized with this scripture why my life never seemed to sustain a joyful contentment.

Emotionally, if you become unattached, this causes discord, tension and a distance will grow. Have you ever felt like you needed to talk to a girlfriend or boyfriend but could not find the way to bridge that mass of disconnect? Eventually this lifestyle will cause you to wake up next to someone you have been with for years and think, I do not even know who you are anymore. What once was two has no become a couple of ones. We need to express not suppress ourselves. This is a partnership. There will always be struggles and obstacles but engage each other and work together with love. We know by our emotions that we care. Do not allow numbness in your relationship. This is almost a deadly silence. Communicate and express yourself in a positive manner as much as possible.

GOODNESS

MASCULINITY, FEMININITY, AND THE FULLNESS OF GOD

A relationship can be looked upon like the ocean.

See many people want to look at relationships in a black and white context. This is unfortunate and wrong. All women, for example, are not looking for a lion. In the same sense, all men are not looking for a beautiful lamb.

I have a friend that had this perspective. We debated frequently about this topic. Until the day came when I asked him, "Do you believe God created us in His image? And do you believe we are wonderfully and fearfully made?" he replied with a yes! So, I said, "well then you must understand and believe we are unique and intricately designed." Again, he agreed but with the counter question "Do you believe in one masculinity and one femininity?" Yes, but there is much more beneath the surface.

There are many types of men and women that can be categorized into a certain personality type. We also can have some of the same characteristics and are able to relate to each other by life's trials and circumstances that are similar. Nevertheless, how we cope or produce reactions will differ. The scars and laugh lines are never the same. We are unique. No two live the same. Therefore, one type of woman does not fit all men nor does one certain type of man fit all women.

This leads me back to looking at the ocean. A relationship, rather man or woman, can be gazed upon in the same way. We can plainly see the ocean is vast, deep, and blue thus needing much exploration just to experience or learn a miniscule amount of what the ocean possesses. This is true with relationships as well. It is physically impossible to know all there is to know about the opposite gender, even your specific love interest. All successful relationships possess the cognitive ability to learn and yearn for their partner.

We are ever evolving and everyday creates new parts of wisdom, wounds, and whimsical circumstances that we learn from and inherit further layers of complexities as a human being. Becoming aware of this reality of your loved one should give you peach and the desire to engage daily with your spouse. Every day is a blessing, and nothing should be taken for granted. This revelation is also backed by the verse from Ephesians 5 :31, A man will leave his father and mother, be united to his wife and the two will become one flesh. Let me put it this way, when you align and love according to God's will, your relationship will feed you daily and you will never deplete the supply of love, learning, and yearning.

There should not be any need to explore or swim deeper into the ocean when there is plentiful to experience right where you wade. Again, I will put emphasis on God's will and knowing who you are. The requisites help you realize who you are and what you are looking for in whom. It is imperative that relationships are built spiritually first, not physically. All requisites are important but there is an order of how to build a relationship. One that works.

This leads me back to the masculinity/femininity discussion with my friend. If we were all the same, then we could continuously exchange in and out people as we see fit. In addition, all relationships would work. Statistics prove that wrong. Divorce is at an all-time high because we try repeatedly to build the relationship outwards to inwards. When it is the exact opposite that is the key to success. True happiness starts with the spirit. When one begins spiritually to learn and grow with another, you will find out long before if you are capable of exceptional love. One should follow the requisites in this order: spiritually, mentally, intimately, emotionally, and physically to build a relationship. The Bible states, that you join flesh and two become one. That should be the last step. Because all else work to align a relationship to succeed. Relationships built on a physical requisite alone never last. No matter how great the attraction. This is the concept of masculinity and femininity. "I am mand and you are woman mantra." Men are not all lions and women are not all lambs. We are not playing some video game called The Hunter and Hunted.

There are many women that have been scorned in battered relationships. My experience with speaking with many of these women who I have come into contact within transition housing and women shelter, have much different views on what they are looking for in a man. Pseudo lions have frightened and attacked these women so often that they want quite the opposite. From an animal perspective, these ladies would feel much safer and find enough provision in a flamingo or antelope. These types still standout yet is graceful without unneeded hostility. These personas are comfortable in crowds. Even still others would desire the intellectual type of the dolphin or the ever-communicating raven. These types are talkative and can speak and express their concerns. Most women would much rather talk it out than fight it out, debate not demand.

From the man's perspective the same applies. Foxes always gain our attention with their prowess and captivating looks. There are men, however, who have been scourged by foxes and have now evolved and involuntarily changed what they are looking for to fulfill their needs. I prefer the javelina or lioness because of the family unit style. These types are also attentive and hardworking.

My hope for you is the realization of the several types of fish in the sea. Accepting that not all well suited for each other and having enough respect for yourself and others to follow an outline that God approves to be the way to a blessed union. Utilizing the knowledge, I hope you gain from the relationship requisites. Finally learning to value your needs in a partner and becoming effective by being selective and that you cherish what you have or honor others and yourself enough not to carry on giving and leaving a part of yourself while taking a part of someone else with every pitstop relationship. Stop this hurtful cycle and reward yourself.

SELF-CONTROL

I would love to convince everyone that my marriage is one with perfect harmony and communication throughout. I will not even try though, because that statement would be as far removed as the east is from the west. In fact, my relationship would more mirror a freeway with traffic congestion and detour signs committing me to the long way around to the destination I desire.

This causes much frustration within my being because I know my peach is the perfect woman for me and our relationship is centered on our faith. Nevertheless, our flesh is sinful. Furthermore, the enemy is effective at using our weaknesses. Conflict occurs when a weakness of two individuals collide. Self-control is crucial for spiritual success as well as your relationships.

I will give an example of the importance of self-control. My wife and I tend to over analyze a lot. Analyzing, is not problematic but compounded with our fleshly will to control situations stirs a vicious mixer to consume. Drinking this concoction usually will breakdown communication. Then leading to speculation of the other's agenda and thoughts. This occurs as irrational tension and anger rears after the initial hurt. Arguments can escalate quickly in this type of dispute, indifferent upon the topic. However, self-control is an overcomer and defeats escalation every time and in any situation. That does not mean we will, in the moments we lose our focus on who that person is and the promises we made to them, a possession of our sinful nature penetrates and perpetuates thinking patterns of our worldly selves of old. The Book of Galatian's chapter five takes roll call of the evil characters, like selfish ambition. This character deceives you into thinking you are God and knows what is best. Commencing to have us voice exactly what is needed to make our spouse a better creation. First, nobody can improve upon God's finest creation made in His image. Secondly, when someone engages you on what you need to fix during a conflict, the advice offered is not for the betterment of you, as much as it is for their own selfish ambitions. Self-control is achieved only by denying the flesh, focusing on positive attributes, controlling your tongue despite thoughts, and trusting god, that He is sovereign over your relationship. A marriage cannot grow up and become the blessed union, if we spend all our time coming down on our spouse because of our own self-doubt.

PRACTICE SELF-CONTROL NOT SPOUSE-CONTROL!!!

GENTLENESS

HEBREWS 12:27

"HOW WHEN ALL ELSE FAILS OR SHAKEN ONE THING WILL REMAIN."

One morning sitting in my bed I caught an episode of Joyce Meyer on TV. I listen to her often, for she is the best when putting a practical spin on our Christianity. This certain episode Joyce had mentioned scripture Hebrews 12:27 "How when all else fails or is shaken one thing will remain, the spirit. As I reflected, on my conviction and everyone else struggling in relationships made me ponder solutions.

Let's use storms to metaphorically exemplify trials within relationships. For instance, hurricanes of infidelity, earthquakes of financial strain, and twisters of confusion. These giant relationship killers: adultery, bankruptcies, home defaults, and communication collapse. However, my thoughts were not about those issues. The conviction I felt came through microburst monsoon cells in the desert. Meaning, that mundane badgering our spouses and loved ones incur is more than menacing, it's damaging.

Spouses are not the rock in which we stand. The great I Am declared, "When thou are weak, I am strong ". In relationships, we tend to rain down on our partners not thinking of the effect it's having physically, mentally, emotionally, spiritually, and intimately. From time to time, certainly it's fair to vent. Although, we must be careful not to let a routine form that leads to misunderstandings, breakdown in communication, and behavioral outbursts. These rumbles of thunder are harmless, but the danger lies in the lightning strikes that follow. Eventually, the strongest partner will get jolted. Once zapped, this can become an emergency. Relationally speaking.

My wife and I are strange in being alike in many areas such as early to rise people. Which also synchronizes are downtimes. Not a good thing to have in common. A relationship needs to be able to overcome moments of weakness and rely on what is true, faithfulness. The evidence of things hoped for and the faith in things unseen. However, we have a different story. We can be consumed with ourselves involuntarily, due to exhaustion or sleep deprivation, for example.

It's a moment like this when unaware your partner might be feeling neglected or even rejected through lack of awareness, which causes disaster.

Silence is golden but not to a relationship, it's deadly. The couple that does not communicate well eradicate. My wife and I do our best to keep focus on recognizing disturbances by each other or outside sources. Often with overkill, allowing our concern to turn to paranoia and cause other issues. Nevertheless, it is better to ask than to avoid. Avoiding a person or their problem never resolves the issue. This type of Coexistence allows the problem to inflate. So, accept that every moment might not bring a perfect partner. Try to hold to the core of a union, love. 1st John 4:16 states, "God is love."

That love looks like this: not holding accountable the partner when flaws are relevant, letting go of the notion of a perfect relationship, and allowing the partnership to gracefully exist. This is done by forgiveness of the spouse and the courage to stay humble in the fire. Never allowing yourself to be fooled into putting the mate on a pedestal where their bound to fall from when the next low-pressure system arrives. The throne is His alone.

Finally, show gentleness like the Father does us, when we know their wrong or have really went too far this time. God allots all of us mercy and grace and so should we our significant. Then after a time of renewal, revisit the issue and repair gently what's damaged.

Lastly, do not let the mundane daily grind turn into an issue that does not exist. All because of over analyzing a partner's exhaustion with paranoia and not practicality. Do not let a "Flesh Flood" wash away your spirit filled campfire. Love is not an emotion it is the union of two spirits intertwined and led to become one led by the One King.

My prayer for anyone out there that cannot recognize each new person that crosses their path as a special creation made by God is for vision of innocence. Allowing all persons to get past first impressions or noticeable flaws according to worldly standards. Further, lord I pray for a washing away of painful memories caused by sin which are truly the root of conflict and judgement. Release these people of this bondage and let them receive a calming patience with every decision made here on out. In Jesus name we ask, Amen.

PATIENCE

1ST SAMUEL 16:7

LOOKS AT THE SURFACE OF A HUMAN AND THE LORD LOOKS AT THE HEART.

How often do we find ourselves being captivated by the way a person looks? How quick are we to jump to a conclusion about a person and their lifestyle? This includes examples like what is she wearing or what does he drive? I wonder what his friends are like, what type of job does she have, why doesn't the hair style I pay for turnout the way she has hers? I imagine sometimes, just how many relationships throughout life, personally speaking, I have skipped over by making a swift conclusion utilizing only my first impressions.

The Lord never falls victim to this shallow way of viewing his creation. He, in fact, takes it to the center of the matter when dealing with us, the heart. We have all heard the ole saying "Never judge a book by the cover". This is an arduous task to be upheld without the Holy Spirit. Man is simply weak when battling the judgement of others or prematurely deciding who the internal person is using external vision. Occurrences, of this nature are birthed because the flesh seeks instant gratification. Recognition and asking for a daily filling of the Holy Spirit is a key prayer request, indeed. God's spirit possesses the characteristics of His true nature which are the fruits. Patience is what we are needing here when engaging with an old song we dance to.

For Samuel warns us of classifying and qualifying others to be labeled and placed in a subgroup. This comes down to what we are feeding ourselves and what is leading us down the path. What's frightening is that the wrong compass allows your outward appearance to show a God complex. Breaking news, you are not God! Even, if you are filled with the Holy Spirit and possess every spiritual gift available.

So, I propose the question to all of you, what is it you are promoting? Is it the flesh or the spirit that navigates your life and how quickly you we decide who they are with a shallow mind and a hollow heart? Let us all commit to be mindful of our own character giving every person the benefit of the doubt. I know it sounds crazy because we are all aware that not everyone is innocent till proven guilty. Surprise! Not one person is. This includes you and I as well. Unless our walk is the better road with God. All good stems from God nowhere else. There are some things even though we are Christ centered and we are his temple. People who gain the ability to grasp the concept and accept a truth are going to receive a blessing bringing so much steadfast resilience when needed to contend with tribulations and conflict. Patience is power that brings peace to your lives. Resting assuredly God's promise. Patience allows you the ability to learn and gain wisdom through restraint in desperate situations on any level. Understanding, God holds all things together and will make it work for those who are called. Being honest though, I cannot say I have earned the control over my emotions which has caused much strife. My flesh and sinful past are to blame not God. Nevertheless, provision of His characteristic called patience is there for all of us. Waiting for us to grasp this amazing ability and fruit that gives way to another. Taking you deeper into a relationship that cherishes moments with the almighty and most high.

FRUITS OF MATURATION

- **PATIENCE**
- **GENTLENESS**
- **SELF-CONTROL**
- **GOODNESS**
- **KINDNESS**

These are a need to proceed to the fruits of freedom. Combined they are the embodiment of the holy spirit. Let me tell you a secret, exuding all nine fruits simultaneously, I doubt man in flesh can sustain for any duration. Despite, how wonderful that would be! This, we are told to ask for, a daily filling of the holy spirit. Skeptic or Christian becomes depleted with every waking moment in the world. It is as if we rise like the sun and full of the spirit, just to succumb to nightfall full of sin. Thank God for His mercy and our ability to confess our sins daily. Blessed to receive the cleansing of the precious blood of the Son and then the replenishing of the Spirit. Honestly, maturity is growing pains, just like puberty as a teenager. Skeptic or new believer I assure you the frustration you will endure is well worth the freedom.

ALL ABOUT THE HOLY SPIRIT AND HIS TEMPLE

Body, Mind and Spirit

The body, mind, and spirit aspect of Gods character and our purpose differ from the Christian perspective, vastly. Largely, in a complete role reversal concerning the body, mind, and spirit. Let me explain, in skeptical simplicity, all parts grow the spirit inside. That said, remember if you fall in the category of pondering Skeptic, newborn Christian, or even the struggling believer for years, all will need perseverance, discernment, and humility to learn and enter an intimate relationship with Jehovah. This will happen through trials that test one's obedience, faith, and emotional steadfastness. Usually, in emotional and tempting experiences encountered by you as a person of flesh but now being conformed to His image. Over a course of time your reactions will not be a repeat. The confirmation can be witnessed within yourself by a sense of peace in conflict, outpouring of compassionate works for others, and even an intuitive conviction to act justly or heed wisdoms call. This persona will maintain consistency prior to the next chapter of your journey.

LEARNING THE JOURNEY AND KNOWING JEHOVAH

ALL ABOUT THE HOLY SPIRIT

1. SPIRIT
   MATURATION OF THE SPIRIT

2. MIND (SPIRITUAL RIGIMORTIS)
   HARDENING OF THE HEART

3. BODY
   SERVICES OF SPIRIT

Skeptic Section 3

RELATIONSHIP REFLECTION

All of us have a past, full of varying emotional times. Our character, as a worldly person is molded by these memories. Knowing this information, look at present day relationships you are involved in and ponder how much of days gone, long before you knew your spouse, have caused damage to the relationship. All due, to the pain of things past and not due to current issues. Sure, present day issues need to be handled. Nevertheless, how exaggerated is the magnitude directly related to some other person, place, or situation? When your able to let go and forgive past hurts through God's love, a blessing of wisdom also manifests. That wisdom produces ability to recognize the origin of why a current day problem might be stirring a response or reaction not fitting the crime. This reality strengthens communication in your relationships, which will bring peace and harmony among your marriages and relationships.

Maturation through reflection of the past comes from accountability and inviting the Lord to lead you. Now I know some are saying I don't need God to do this, and maybe you are correct. However, I know personally, that my personality defects caused by poor choices or worldly desire can be found, exposed, and disposed of much quicker in Jesus name. As an intelligent man, why, would I refuse that kind of helping hand?

DEGREE TO SIN

In my opinion, a ladder of severity exists with sin. First, let me acknowledge to all of you that I know all sins are forgiven equally, thanks to the works of the cross. For the skeptic reading this, it might seem a no brainer to differences in wrongdoings to others having a different degree of severity.

My reasons for this belief are biblically minded and not driven by worldly nature though. Elaborating, the degree of sin differs because of where it resides and it's point of impact. Some sin or pain hurts more than others which proves a degree. What doesn't change is the healing or forgiving. For example, an injury from an accident or a game you recover from with time but when you do, it's finished. Furthermore, there isn't a halfway to forgiveness, not true forgiveness. As a Christian, I'm thankful for that because my eternity would rest on me then, just like yours does without God.

Skeptic, I would like to ask you a couple of questions that you can answer among yourselves. Why are you holding that grudge or refusing to accept a God that wants to love you and tell you it's ok? Where is the defiance coming from, that keeps you from His full capability of helping rid, you of the walls built by the sinful acts committed against the body (Paul eludes) to in the New Testament?

BROKENNESS

Defining moments, we all have them, right? Some, might be downright overwhelming. Well, here is a little truth for you, moments do not define you, as a Christian, God uses them to refine you. Just as a mustang must broken for a smoother ride, we also must endure a rough time or few to mature. When the realization happens and we acknowledge to God we need help, it's at that point of crying out that many encounter the Lord and His amazing grace. Skeptics, can you imagine having a freedom from your brokenness? God can do this for you and in this remove the hardness holding your heart.

When this occurs through true vulnerability and exposure, ones eyes will begin to see and their ears hear what's been there all along waiting. The awareness of our flaws and sins and the pain we've inflicted and been afflicted by can bring a release from the hurt and guilt. When we confront and confess, our repentance brings the healing hands of God that cleanses us of the world's mud caked to our flesh. Skeptics, the feeling is like none other you've ever known. You'll walk lighter, the day will seem brighter, and the chokehold from sin and the world will be demanded to loosen its grip and finally, you'll breathe again.

REDEMPTION NOT RETALIATION

I spent many a day hiding from demons and using my past as the justifiable reason. The fear I held from the torment, neglect, and abuse bestowed by the people I sought were the factors for the fear. During this portion of my life, the only friend I could find that consistently showed up was abandonment.

This friend accompanied me well into my adulthood, allotting me an excuse to retaliate any time I felt pain or threatened in a relationship. Life truly was awful and full of frustration daily in most of my relationships. Even worse, was the duration of this cycle that lasted even after my conversion. I couldn't find a reason why. Over and over through self talk, I declared my love for God and finally, I listened spiritually and received the revelation that I struggled with accepting fully, my new identity and struggled because of the large part of my life that I leaned on my past as a crutch of definition. Thus, causing my frustration and abuse others incurred on my behalf. Moreover, my stinking thinking was terrorizing my wife all because I couldn't figure out who I was in Christ.

Friends, there isn't an easy road to take when your past is checkered like a flag waving on the last lap of race day. It took many prayers, patience, and fortitude through many hard conflicts to gain the knowledge of who I really am because of what Jesus has done for me here on earth and continues to do from the throne.

Currently, I've learned how to re-center and lean into Him instead of that PAST crutch when I start to stumble in my relationships. The fear has faded in many ways and I've grown more confident in my identity in Christ. This has blessed me with many opportunities to help others and build positive relationships. I now can accept the truth that anyone can and will disappoint me or even hurt me sometimes, but the good news is Christians don't abandon they return to mend what's been wounded. All possible, because God's love never fails. His love had the key to release me from the bondage.

"DON'T HAVE ANYTHING TO DO WITH FOOLISH AND STUPID ARGUMENTS BECAUSE YOU KNOW THEY PRODUCE QUARRELS."

We have all been in a situation where we have lost control of our tongue and emotions.

Nothing is resolved when you are irrational or led by an emotional response. There are two key fruits involved in being successful at this approach in your relations: self-control and patience.

I have many examples, as we all do, but I will use a situation that occurred recently, surprisingly in a Bible study. Another brother and I were reading a study that was a bit full of passion. He was on fir speaking about the righteousness we receive when we accept Jesus as our Savior. I wanted to continue forward about the righteousness being demonstrated through our works. HE refused to allow me to delve into the works. I know now that he was afraid of the confusion that might stir from our listeners. However, to them, I felt shut out and my feelings were hurt. It is ok for Christians to disagree but not when leading others. There is a time and place. I maintained but not until we had made everyone feel uncomfortable. I quieted myself a little too late. Thus, leading to a disrupted session which inhibited the Spirit to move. Our pride took over. That is always a bad outcome, pride only breeds quarrels and restraint one can find wisdom.

So, take Solomon's advice along with Paul's: most times as you feel your blood pressure rising and your heart begging to race, you are about to enter a race that doesn't have a victory at the end of it. All parties involve are headed for a collision. One that is going to call you back to repair the damage that could have been avoided if you would have just controlled your tongue.

EXIT THE BROKEN ROAD

> ### 1ST JOHN 3:6
>
> NO ONE WHO LIVES IN HIM KEEPS ON SINNING. NO ONE WHO CONTINUES TO SIN HAS EITHER SEEN HIM OR KNOWN HIM.

This verse is immensely powerful. Still it can also be misunderstood. We are all sinners and will continue to sin. The difference is in the nature and frequency of the sin. Along with sin as a lifestyle, the old self passes away and is a new creation when you confess that Jesus Christ is Lord and recognize and believe that he hung on the cross to pay the debt for all of our sins and rose again 3 days later. Amen.

That being said, there will be slip ups with different things from time to time; however, you will not be to live in sin (lifestyle) The sins also will not engulf you mind or heart to the point of it being possessive.

In my own experience, once this calling to come home to your Lord and Savior happens, it is impossible to carry on with the old you. Sure, there is wrought to be done in me. There always will be. It is just that the Holy Spirit that is living inside me is grieved by sins. The Lord will deliver me from addictions, habits, and whatever else I cannot handle. The rest will come with the walk. I had issues with drugs and alcohol. These almost instantly vanished, my desires changed. My heart yearned for a strong relationship with God. I wanted Him to be happy with me, till do. I craved His word like spiritual milk. I need to be fed. The Spirit inside me was alive and working. To this day it remains the same and even stronger. I continue to grow in my Faith.

Your spiritual senses will develop, and your fruit will bear. It is just not possible to do both. You cannot serve the flesh (sin) and serve the (spirit) Lord. Yes, sin will co and then God he sent his son to pay the price for them, but we will be at peace with God and ask forgiveness of those. Then continue down the path towards righteousness being led by our Heavenly Father. It is not possible to be engrossed in sin, whatever that sin might be lust, fornication, pornography, drugs, alcohol, pride, etc. and serve God. For you were made alive in Christ even when you were dead in your transgressions.

Skeptic Section 2

RELATIONSHIP, RESPECTFULLY

A relationship in right standing consists of doing it opposite of the Hollywood model or instant gratification. There are five requisites that make up a person. Each one of those must become familiar to you in what your own makeup is and what you truly need in turn to be the best version of you. Not adhering to the effort and time needed to learn will result in many of worldly relationships that will crumble. Simply starting with the foundation, that requisite is spiritual.

Spiritual insight is imperative to knowing yourself and what is required from a relationship to reach that fullness of a union. God also wants that for us as well. The very first book of the Bible God declares, "It's not good for man to be alone" (Genesis2:18). Today's world does not see it that way, though. Instant gratification and outward appearances drive the person absence of the spirit. How foolish can one be? To exclude the one who created everything and everyone from being a component of the relationship process is a guarantee of struggle and failure at love. 1st John 4:16 tells us directly God is love. Therefore, without His spirit a relationship cannot have love present. It is that simple. A filling of the Holy Spirit even in just one spouse can produce love that is sustainable. Due to Gods attributes present in conduct.

Next up would be a combination of two requisites being processed simultaneously. The mental and the physical will come to the front. I would love to leave the physical for last, but it truly seems impossible for most. So, if we can begin to at least stabilize the desires and put some boundaries up to protect us from our fleshly desires, we at least improve and show respect for God, ourselves, and counterparts. Although, physical beauty is a temptress like none other, we can focus ourselves on the activities and common interests in hobbies, careers, interests, goals, and culinary pleasures, for example. This can keep one busy and distracted somewhat from cravings of sexual desire. I am not saying sex is awful or bad, even. We just need to refrain from giving it the lead in making our choices in relationships. Despite anyone's belief, a relationship cannot survive on flesh alone. The spirit, mental, and physical all need to be quenched and fed appropriately. Furthermore, aligned with Gods will in accordance with His word. Mental stimulation is an amazing way to divert your focus upon other commonalities and even pet peeves might get discovered that you realize are unbearable for you to continue a relationship quest with the individua (I mean ferrets, 3 of them). In doing so, both people, in this scenario can exit with respect intact. But if the like is genuine and a feeling of enjoyment flares when your near one another or even anticipation when time is drawing.

The final two requisites also can pair up and tend to alert with surprise. Often, it is unlikely until the moment is at hand to respond. One might recognize an ex who is out with a new partner, or that I lack ability to empathize with them and their addictive personality, because I do not have any experience myself. Intimacy, and emotional requisites directly derive from past experiences of hurts, achievements, and the spiritual requisite growth. If a person cannot relate to a circumstance or feeling, then there will be a disconnect in that relationship and its maturation. That is unless proper relational health and discipline is being followed. Then there would be a possible interceding of Gods spirit guiding you or them in a way to bring necessary words of affirmation or even intuitive action that can be taken to show and offer proper care to whatever situation, in addition, to being genuine. Have you ever just said the right thing at the right time? Then wonder, where did that come from? How about, obliviously, arriving at your destination realizing the last 5 minutes of the drive, you were in a daydream of disastrous probability. It is amazing what God can do through the spiritual requisite to intervene and assist you or others around you. In turn, we learn how to love, trust, respect, and administer the right relational medicine for the moment.

Let me assure you that this is a broad overview of the spiritual, mental, physical, emotional, and intimate makeup of a human being made by divine design with a purpose. Communication is the universal tool in relationships. Efficient listening and respectful response are the manifestation of communication. Never once doubt, mastering this tool is not important. Even if you have done all your homework and been obedient to Gods design of marriage. Matured in all areas and reached full enlightenment of what you can offer and need in a relationship. All relationships require maintenance just like vehicles. They will still breakdown just like a mechanics truck if he does not put gas in it, air the tires up, give it a tune up from time to time. Like the mechanic and his truck, a relationship can get a flat tire with a harsh word spoken but unintentional, Still careless, and rude just the same. Encounter a need to replace the air filter due to anxiety striking with unforeseen sickness .For example, worry can zap one's ability to breathe in a relationship which can wear the engine out of the person being questioned constantly due to insecurity delivered as worry. A time might occur where the relationship runs out of gas because the same fast paced routine has lost its luster and ability to captivate your eyes and ears anymore leaving your spouse unaware of your loneliness and need for a changeup and quality time.. However, mature relationships with strong requisite health recognize and dissolve of any damaging dilemmas. Tension and conflict are certain but diligent effort from both partners can overcome. **Come what may,** is a phrase my wife and I use to acknowledge our commitment to relate, reconcile, and restore our relationship and I promise we have had our share of rocky roads that rerouted us on our Journey.

WHO AM I TALKING TO WHEN NO ONE IS AROUND?

1 THESSALONIANS 5:17

"PRAY INCESSANTLY"

Prayer might at first thought, come off as an easy concept. I mean we all pray or complain from time to time to God, believer, or skeptic just the same. To many, reading this right now, this might surprise you when I inform you are doing it wrong. Or at least, not the way Our father in heaven desires us to do so. We truly need to be in constant communication with our Father. In a comparable way to how we seek out our partner for advice or companionship. The lord delights in our yearning for Him, whatever the cause. How awesome is it to have a wonderful and perfect being chasing after our time when He lives outside of conceptual time?

Prayer for God is as communication is for us. We share the joyful surprises and awful struggles with our partners, don't we? No problem fighting through frustrating disappointments and even taking it out on the partner who is our safehouse away from the world or should be. What we typically take to the significant other that happened in the day, should also include the Father. First, by giving praise for all you have inherited and such. Then the glory due for His creation. Finally, praying for others and then your petitions. Bringing Him up to date with your petitions by discussing it with Him might seem to escape the ritual but I digress, Prayer does not mean you have to be formal all the time. Prayer can come in many forms. Just as we speak to our family and loved ones in different approaches and moods. The lord visions everyone we can and should do the same with the Father. Remember we are his bride. Sometimes we talk to him as a Father, other times it could be as a friend, confidant, brother, advisor, counselor, comforter, and even as a king. God can even be intimate with you. He wants a real, deep, meaningful relationship with you. Give it to Him and you will receive the greatest love man could ever know. Rather you are at home alone in bed or walking in the park with you family or at the office surrounded by employees and co-workers or down on your knees at the altar of your church. Talk to Him. Pray continually.

WITHSTANDING WORLDLY WAYS

PHILLIPIANS 4:13/2ND CORINTHIANS 9:8

"WE CAN DO ALL THINGS THROUGH HIM WHO GIVES ME STRENGTH"

What you speak, you bring forth. Focus your energy on the positive rather than the negative. In today's times we are saturated with technology and avenues of communication: emails, phones, televisions, radios, computers, Facebook, Instagram etc. On the surface, these are great inventions and discoveries. These are used to transfer or divulge information to mass populous or individuals. However, we become absent minded on all the negative banter we receive. See in today's world people involuntarily hang on the next headline of negativity. The next drama unfolding in movie stars' lives. The next international threat or dispute. The next collapse of an economy. The next corruption, deceit, demise, death, or devastation to the birthed into the world. All this verbal manure that we ingest saps us of our energy. In today's world, we have so many people depressed and on medication, overweight and insecure, hopeless and without purpose. We must become cognitive of what is being fed to us just for the sake of ratings. If you take life as a vehicle you are not going to get extremely far in reverse (negativity). Put your life in gear and drive forward (positivity). In doing so, you can diminish the intake of what bogs you down. Be inspired, search out stories of achievement, overcoming, and conquering. Be alert in all you feel body, soul, and mind. There is a diet for all three parts of humanity. I am going to hand on the word race because that is how we should perceive this life. So, get in your car and drive forward. Race towards the finish, setting out to achieve your dreams and goals. Do not let anyone or outlet fill you with all the evil and failures. Believe in yourself and the creator. Phil 4:13 tells you that you can do all things through him. Know that you are loved and blessed. Get up, get out, and go for it. 2nd Corinthians 9:8 tells us that in all works we will do good. Thus, being successful according to the grace God abounds to us. I will leave you with this promising affirmation to live by: do not be guided by man's negativity. Be directed by God's positivity.

BEYOND

COLOSSIANS 3:23

WHATEVER YOU DO, WORK AT IT WITH ALL YOUR HEART, AS WORKING FOR THE LORD, NOT FOR MEN.

This verse is offered to us in the manner of how we should conduct ourselves concerning matters of the family, friends, and colleagues. When we interact with anyone, it should be done with respect and consideration for the matter at hand without allowing our emotions to lead us in a direction that would lead the person(s) to alter their intent in the conversation. Thus, causing the person(s) to cater to our view or sensitivity in the topic. This takes full dedication to be the best listener. But his is what Paul is asking of us in the sense of discussion.

Let us continue with actions that include work, play, church function and various other tasks. When we engage in anything the Lord wants us to put all our heart into it. Which makes sense, why does anyone do anything half-hearted? Only because you do not want to do it and/or are forced to do so. If this is true, you are only being dishonest with yourself and whomever else is involved, which, in turn, becomes a disservice that goes against what a Christian is called to do in service. Therefore, we should approach all matters with a full and pure heart, dedicated to seeing it through or be kinds enough to decline or step away from the task, conversation, relationship, or job.

UNSELFISH ACTS OF RECONCILIATION

2ND CORINTHIANS 7:10

"GODLY SORROW BRINGS REPENTANCE THAT LEADS TO SALVATION AND LEAVES NO REGRET, BUT WORLDLY SORROW BRINGS DEATH."

Obviously, directed towards the sinner reaching a point of turn his life over to God. The best thing anyone can do is turn to the Lord and ask for forgiveness leading to the greatest gift-the gift of salvation.

However, if you delve deeper into the scripture and acknowledge how many times we attempt to fix or resolve issues with an apology. Meanwhile we continue to do what caused the hurt feelings we apologized for. This is because we are being sorrowful in a worldly way. Sure, we want to resolve the issue at hand, but we do not want to change anything about ourselves to make it happen. We are simply mouthing an apology not from eh heart. It is kind of like feeding empty calories. The ones with no nutritional value. You are ingesting but not investing in what is needed. So, what is being served up does not serve a purpose. True sorrow is filled with humility and willingness to do what is necessary to find peace. Returning to love and allowing the joy to come back. Who is right or wrong becomes irrelevant int his earnest repentance and sorrow? We are simple and genuinely concerned in the mending of the relationship. Relationship is what it is all about. Relationship with God and with others.

Skeptic Section 1

INTROSPECTION TO DIRECTION

A few offerings of insightful knowledge of something else might have had a part in that situation. Even more, a lesson in direction and accountability. Including, a sense of dignity done right. Whatever that means, right? Sarcasm aside skeptic, these positive attributes and tools when used are invaluable. Experiences with these brought a realization much later, concerning my inability to utilized or display in most of my life. I as well as the next skeptic would have given extraordinarily little credit to anyone or thing for something I did or believed to have the control and complete decision process upon my shoulders. I did not chalk it up to luck, intuition, or even some stars aligned horoscopic notion. In hindsight, some moments seem way to coincidental, even back when it happened, to ignore. These periods of stirring my mind to question what just happened would feel eerie and a presence of something more that had a hand in the outcome and how I responded. Although, back then, it seemed to fade quickly after the ordeal or circumstance. I bet most of the skeptics out there reading this have a few stories that could not be explained. That shock you felt, or others witness and asked, "Who are you and where is my_____", (fill in whatever title fits the moment). I encourage all of you to meditate on this and attempt to recall at least one ominous circumstance of divine intervention or happenings not typical of your character. This is an interceding or a testimony to draw you near, perhaps. After a while when the Spirit has opportunity to teach, prayer, forgiveness, discernment, and effort become commonplace to your demeanor not small miracles.

SKEPTIC PROLOGUE

For the skeptic who makes the decision ***Our Journey is not an Accident*** is worth the read, thank you. Your inquisitive nature towards religion or directly Christianity, perhaps will be worth it. The journey you are beginning augers a unique invitation to both Christian and skeptic of all levels of experience.

Personally, it's my hope to bring both groups together and find a peaceful approach in education, acceptance, and willingness to get past the delivery of some churches, concerning Christian faith and realize the love of God is large enough to welcome us all into His home. I truly know many people that are and were turned off and sent in a different direction, due solely, because of the delivery of the gospel. Not all of us can hear of the fiery torment awaiting us if we refuse to submit to Christian conversion, immediately. Scare tactics and forceful assaults upon us like the action transpiring in a UFC octagon will not be welcomed by all. I do not recall Jesus screaming of a person's demise and becoming irrational with those who opposed His ways. Quite the opposite, self-control, kindness, and friendship to the wretched tended to be the common demeanor of Jesus. There are so many people who go through days, weeks, and months of their lives with the absence of notoriety, or a notion of kindness. Even more that truly do not have anyone to visit or call up to console or confide in as one would do a friend.

Skeptics, ***Our Journey is not an Accident*** is going to speak of the Christian faith and walk, as one might expect. That is not the entirety of what can be ingested. Love and kindness can be experienced despite a decision by anyone, through readings of my own humbling failures and endeavors exposed and shared within. The practical wisdom alone is worth the read and acknowledging that a better road is available to anyone. In full disclosure, I walked for forty years down paths without direction. It did not appear awful all the time, either. However, nothing that seemed good ever was sustainable and when life did throw a curveball or collapse, it hit hard and the fall hurt.

The last incident that happened destroyed all resonance of what I called my life and others as well. Some that would never have another opportunity to change directions. My rock bottom that finally broke my prideful ego of a very functional and enjoyable but worldly existence caused many emotions like grief, anger, sadness, confusion, and fear from dozens of people. No man could fix what I had broken much less restore. To this day I do not know the outcome for all affected but by God's grace I had been redirected.

D.R. Birch

How much desire beneath this shell of my being does it take to say, all is swell!

Everyone is aware the world is facing the consequences of poor decisions by our leaders. Then add the impact to people all over the world adjusting to a new way of existing, the outlook is one of fear and skepticism. 2020 has opened many portals for sin and its vessels of evil to devour. Plagues, war, violence, famine, and death are here and in the face of us all. Being skeptic or faithful follower is irrelevant in the world at this moment. However, it's crucial if in fact, we are experiencing the tribulations. Therefore, it's imperative to take time and search within, to make certain, one is at peace, if this journey is approaching its final hours.

Our Journey is not an Accident was written to bring forth a mentality of an overcomer. To hopefully restore optimism in difficult times. To help people searching for new paths or to get back on the right track. A hope restored and faith finder assistant. This outlook hasn't changed.

The world did though, with intensity and velocity. These uncertain days have not led me to still waters either. During the Covid-19 stage of life, past months have delivered a loss of a friend & business partner, breakdowns in my marriage, loss of employment, separation from other believers, and poor choices because of not going to the well when I had been thirsty. Deciding to face issues of any severity, without God's guidance, is foolish and leads to further complications.

Life is anything but certain with COVID 19. Relationships are being pushed to the brink of dissolution made possible by the stressors that existed already within the relationships. Social structure for families has been compromised. As business owners stand defenseless while forced to watch their dreams and financial means burned to the ground by other citizens crying out for stability and equality. Our government has had their mask of valiant and ominous demeanor exposed for its real face. A face that declares a flag of surrender to COVID and its consequences. Then there is the media salivating to release the next piece of exaggerated context of a statement, bloated statistics to cause anxiety, or useless information to sway the attention of viewers away from the truth. Every person of office declares to have the solution to the pandemic and/or answers to equality awarded and sustained for all people. Well, we the people are waiting.

Unfortunately, the horizon is missing the light. The light which is God. This is the reason struggle continues but then there is a chance that it is the will of God. Not just an allowance by the creator for maturation and evolution through the consequences of sin. Either way will leave severe devastation and people scouring for safety.

My life Has changed completely. The outward appearance does not look the same. Still, everyone that has relations with me that carries concern or believes I've lost hope, don't. The bounce-back is greater than the beatdown when God is your corner-man.

So, to all those people without God, now is the time to work-out your salvation with fear and trembling. Don't waste any more precious time. Believers that are suffering and looking for answers, earnestly pray, practice the fruits, and let your actions not words declare it, for He is coming soon. Finally, to skeptics on the fence heed the call to take cover because the predicament to live indecisively and accepting everything without a moral stand is foolish and costly in ways unfathomable.

Christians, remain steadfast knowing this too will work for the greater good for all called according to His purpose. Our family friend from the "Woman Blessed by the Well" chapter, is caught in a battle that seems to never end. Her son that fought cancer and was healed by the glory of God is now on a ventilator like so many but I assure all reading this, the fight is not over. This lady hasn't wavered and is not complaining about why God but instead asking, what God needs her to do. Declaring His will to be done and confirming the promise to us, still is alive and guaranteed.

ABOUT THE AUTHOR

D.R. Birch, a fresh author who offers a rare opportunity to delve into a book that's relatable. Rather, skeptic or christian D.R. will meet you at your trial or triumph. He is a man with vast life struggles that would overwhelm most people. However, since his faith arose God has replaced overwhelm with overcome. Which has inspired D.R. to a life of sharing the promise. D.R. is married, has four teenagers, and lives in Missouri. He is currently finishing a behavioral science degree and studied theology and crisis counseling for two years at Emmaus correspondence School for ministry. In addition, D.R. has obtained  certificates in various areas, sometimes as a student and other times a survivor, including abuse, recovery, anger management, and spiritual direction. D.R. is a chef who loves to play tennis, and visiting new churches.

Printed in the United States
By Bookmasters